At the Sign of the Harlequin's Bat

Dear Pam & Alan.

With love and

best wishes.

Isabelle.

Cyril Beaumont at 68 Bedford Court Mansions. The statuette is of Emma Livry.

At the Sign of the Harlequin's Bat

Isabelle Stoughton

DANCE BOOKS

Published by Dance Books Ltd.,
Charwell House
Wilsom Road
Alton
Hampshire
GU34 2PP

© 2011 Isabelle Stoughton

ISBN 978-1-85273-150-2

A CIP catalogue record for this book is available from the
British Library

Printed and bound in Great Britain by Lightning Source

Dedication

To Sir Peter Wright, dear friend for nearly sixty years and to Sonya, of Blessed Memory.

With thanks to:

Alix Kirsta (Alexandra) for her constant encouragement to write this book and my son Richard and my granddaughter Natasha for dealing with all the technical necessities of present-day book writing in which their ancient forebear is completely illiterate.

CONTENTS

The author, outside 75 Charing Cross Road, c1954.

PROLOGUE

My mother, searching diligently as she did every month through the advertisements on the last pages of *The Bookseller*, suddenly called to me, 'Listen to this – it sounds just right for you!' She read out a sparsely-worded request for help in a bookshop in Charing Cross Road, specialising in books on ballet and theatre. Name and address only given: C W Beaumont, 75 Charing Cross Road, WC2. No telephone number. I fairly rushed for writing paper and pen; I had known that shop for years and C W Beaumont was a legend in the ballet world. I wrote saying that I knew the shop, had been a frequent customer and had been watching ballet for years. Furthermore, I was free to work immediately. In a day or two a letter arrived written on the soon-to-be-familiar red-headed writing paper and bearing a missive in writing so fine and cramped that I could read it only with difficulty – and that was soon to be familiar as well. It asked me to come for an interview the following Friday at 3 o'clock. If I had already had an appointment to see the Queen (who had only just become Queen) I think I would have asked her to postpone it. Lèse-majesté!

From Wimbledon, where I at that time lived with my parents, the journey to Charing Cross Road entailed a ten minute walk to the bus stop, 93 bus to the railway station, Wimbledon to Waterloo on Southern Railway, across to the Underground, then the Northern Line to Leicester

Square and a five minute walk to no. 75. Well over an hour's journey but I regarded it as nothing if only I could work for Cyril Beaumont.

There he was, as I had seen him so often, brown-suited, *en brosse* hair, eyes twinkling through rimless spectacles, ready to see if I would suit him. Although it was early in the afternoon, he shut the shop and locked the door while he took me round. There was not much 'taking round' to be done; the shop was small and crammed with books from floor to ceiling. He looked for my reaction as he detailed several books in a quiet rather dry voice. 'Of course,' he said, 'I shall have to ask my wife before making a decision.' I realised that there was a presence in the background to be deferred to.

Then we moved into the adjoining office. It was minute – a huge desk piled high with papers of all sorts, an enormous and ancient typewriter and an antique 'daffodil' telephone. Mr Beaumont's chair was behind the desk and a leather-seated carver in front for visitors. It was all rather dark and sombre, there being only one sash window looking out onto brick buildings. There was a small gas fire which, my future employer told me, could be lit in very cold weather. It was to become the bane of my life, had I known it.

He looked at me quizzically. I must have looked as though I had entered Paradise because he said: 'I'll show you the basement if you're interested. Mind the stairs.' (I was to hear that warning every day in the years that followed.) Clutching the rail of the daunting spiral staircase, I followed him into the bowels of 75 Charing Cross Road, emerging 15 minutes later. He looked at my enchanted expression and said, 'I don't think I'll bother to ask my wife, when could you start?'

A year later he told me that, having read my letter, he had not answered any of the others he had received. 'Bit naughty of me, I suppose,' he said.

CHAPTER ONE

The shop in 1953 remained largely unchanged from when it had opened in 1910: the same chairs, the same desk and bookshelves, the same decrepit brown linoleum which covered the floor, even – I felt sure – the same dust. I was to become unpleasantly familiar with that ancient dust, when after a week or two spent sizing up what should be done to improve the place I began moving the books and 'dusting' them. Within 24 hours I contracted a sore throat which developed into a raging cough. I refused to take a day off (what shame that would have been), hacking my way through several uncomfortable days. Mr B, noticing, was quite alarmed. When I said my state was due to dust he said, 'It never affects *me*.' Later I found that he had quite severe bouts of bronchitis at least once a year. Nevertheless, dust or no dust, I was determined that several changes would have to be made or I could not see how business could be maintained at any worthwhile level. (What youthful arrogance – the business had been maintained for years.) The first victim of my enthusiasm was the telephone, grey with age and dirt, through which it was barely possible to hear the caller. When I mentioned this to Mr B, he said, 'Well, it works,' thinking, I believe, that the dimly-heard, wavering voices were due to distance and not to the build up of the human detritus of many years. In the end he agreed to let a Post Office engineer call 'just to have a look'. He was not going to commit himself to modernisation without a fight. The young man came and was appalled: 'I've never seen one of these,' he said. A new instrument was ordered and installed within a week. Mr B was highly suspicious, pretending not to know which end to speak into and refusing to answer it at first, calling me to do so, whatever else I might be doing.

The next change was the tidying of the desk, piled six inches high with papers, letters, bills, photographs, magazines and programmes. There was, next to the telephone, a vicious metal spike, on which letters having been answered, had been speared – for eternity it seemed since some of them dated back twenty years. He said he had no trouble with this state of things and when looking for something he thought to be on the desk, he would pass both hands, palms down, over the entire contents, until almost by extrasensory perception he would announce triumphantly, 'Got it' – and sure enough there was the desired item. It did not work for me, however, and I determined to get to grips with the situation. I was very pleased with the result and when Sacheverell Sitwell paid his next visit I begged him to come and see the transformation. GOOD GOD, Cyril,' he said 'IT'S RED!' (meaning the leather with which the desk was covered). 'Yes,' said Mr B resignedly, 'and I can't find a thing.'

There was a tattered old curtain, made of furnishing velvet or brocade or something once grand, which hung by the shop door and was supposed to be drawn before the door was locked for the night. I thought it looked not only unattractive but positively insanitary and was quite keen to remove it. Mr B looked fondly as at an old friend when I took it away to be 'cleaned'. Once freed from its rail and removed from the premises it disintegrated into about twenty ragged pieces. It never came back.

A shelf above Mr B's chair held several piles of brown paper parcels. It transpired that these were a kind of filing cabinet (in the loosest description of that word) and, amazingly, he knew – again with a display of ESP – what each one contained. These were used to check dates, casts, etc when writing the weekly column (column! 250 words quite often) for *The Sunday Times* and were to prove invaluable during the fracas over *The Firebird* which occurred in 1954. But more of that later. Much later.

Other small shelves, to the right of where he sat, contained other packets of goodness-knows-what. All manner of little treasures and memorials and also – surprisingly – little envelopes containing small amounts of money, half-crowns, florins, shillings and sixpences. When I found the first one I mentioned this to Mr B thinking it had been left there by mistake, but no; it was all part of the Beaumont system, as were so many surprising things. One evening, I shut the shop and prepared myself for a visit to the Royal Opera House. Being short of time and having only about threepence in my purse, I borrowed half-a-crown for a taxi. I really do not remember paying it back in all the flurry of business that went on there. Perhaps I still owe it?

The shop itself, so small that three people made a crowd, housed not only scores of books (some there since before the first World War) but a table-top built over the stairs and a shelf where sat the till, a grand affair about a foot-and-a-half high and almost as wide. I cannot, at this distance in time, recall details of its make but I do recall that the pinging of its keys when a sale had been made was a very happy sound for Mr B. There were books on shelves near the ceiling rarely examined and never sold. One day Sacheverell Sitwell was discussing some aspect of art or travel or theatre (exactly which I cannot say). 'I know where I can find a book on that subject,' quoth my employer. Alas, he could not reach the top shelf where the desired book was resident. 'Come here Isabelle,' he said, seizing me round the waist and trying to lift me up. Of course, we both landed in a heap amid gales of laughter and without the book. 'Let me,' said the great Sitwell, 'I'm taller than both of you,' and by stretching one arm he retrieved whatever it was that could not be reached by lesser men (in the matter of height only).

The window was dressed with a selection of new books (that is, they were not second-hand) but although a few got changed when new publications arrived, many of them stayed there until familiarity, as one might say, bred contempt because all the 'regulars' knew about them anyway. This state of affairs did not please me and neither did the meagre lighting of the window which consisted of a low-powered bulb covered by a green metal shade situated on the outside so that after dark very little could be seen of the goods within. It was uphill work to persuade Mr B that we really should have some proper inside illumination installed making the window's contents attractive after dark. This idea rumbled about for some time; references were made to the 'blackout' where darkness in shop windows had been compulsory. I reminded him that the war had been over for nine years and that an attractively-lit window would bring in more customers who actually bought books. 'I'll have to ask my wife', was said as a last resort, but, to my surprise and delight, Mrs Beaumont thought it a good idea and so an electrician was summoned and lights installed. Once having persuaded him that we really should concentrate on making the window look good enough to entice customers in, I began a programme of changing books frequently. After every daring movement of goods, I would call him to come outside and give his approval. 'I'll just get my hat', he would say, even in a heat wave, before donning his broad-brimmed brown fedora-type headgear. He was bothered that I went hatless. 'Mind you don't catch cold,' he would adjure me solemnly, even in the heat of summer.

Outside the shop stood two ancient bookcases which were filled daily with anything not fit to sell in the shop, damaged books, old magazines or anything that, while stopping to look at them, might attract the potential customer inside. Once there they would see how wonderful the shop was and come again. Maybe even buy something.

Attracted by the unusual display of new books, a woman whom I had seen hovering outside for some time, finally came in and somewhat nervously asked Mr B, who was in the shop, the price of a new book. I think it was Haskell's *Gala Performance* (42s). 'Two guineas', he replied promptly. 'Could I possibly have a look at it?' she asked timorously. He had quite obviously taken an instant dislike to this potential customer (which happened sometimes) and made a great fuss over getting the step-ladder and clambering up as if in pain to the level where the book was placed. This was quite unnecessary as there was a copy in the office but he had clearly decided that she should see what trouble she was causing. Placed before her on the table top, *Gala Performance* seemed to send the woman into a trance. 'How much did you say it was?' she asked, playing for time. 'Two guineas', he replied firmly. 'Two guineas', she repeated, as if in wonder. Turning over a few pages she said again 'Two guineas'. At this the proprietor of 75 Charing Cross Road fairly exploded. 'If you say "two guineas' again I shall scream', he said. The woman fled. 'Thank God she's gone.' 'Why did you do that?' I asked him, 'she might have bought it'. 'She had no intention of buying it', he said 'she was just a time-waster. I can get very nasty when I like.' I was to hear that several times in the future.

I mention this only because it was quite contrary to his usual quiet, courteous behaviour. But just occasionally, when something or somebody really annoyed him, we would have such a forthright reaction.

After many months I had reorganised the entire Beaumont establishment. For the first time in years – many years – it was possible to find what one was looking for within a matter of minutes. Mr B, while not entirely approving, since he hated changes and rather liked muddle, gave grudging approval and even a little praise.

Perhaps it is time to return to my least favourite part of 75, the basement and 'Mind the Stairs', the perpetual warning to everyone who came within a foot of the iron spiral staircase. Whatever would today's Health and Safety brigade have made of it? Once down the stairs, one could just make out in the gloom more books, shelves full and piles of them, more brown paper parcels tied with string and then a whole area containing tins of food, jars of fruit, bottles of wine and packets and packets of tea. These had all been sent during or just after the war by kindly overseas friends who knew of the tight rationing in England. So far as I could see, nothing had ever been touched since being unpacked from its parcel. Some of the liquid in the jars was decidedly cloudy and the contents of a packet of tea which I surreptitiously opened was covered in mildew. Holding up a jar of peaches in kirsch while down there looking for something with Mr B, I asked him why he and Mrs Beaumont did not eat some of these delicacies.'Well,' he said, 'we thought they might be rather too rich'. I don't think it ever occurred to them to pass such comestibles on to someone who might not find them so indigestible.

Facing the bottom of the stairs was a door marked WC. It looked sinister to me at first sight and not much better when the door was opened, revealing a very basic water closet and a small hand basin. It was cleaned out once a week by the woman who washed the deplorable brown lino above and even she regarded it with some reserve. 'I reckon they kept a monster in there in the old days,' she said to me once. I could not but agree.

The two men, father and son, who kept the opticians shop next door had to share this doubtful convenience with us, to Mr B's quite obvious displeasure every time one of them should have the temerity to come into our shop and approach the staircase. 'What on earth does *he* want?' he would say to me, even before the poor wretch was out of earshot. After a while I stopped giving the obvious answer.

A man came in one Saturday morning, quite plainly not wanting to buy anything but to look at everything. He must have examined every book within reach and then moved towards the stairs, by which Mr B happened to be standing, and said 'Excuse me, I'd like to look downstairs.' 'I dare say you would,' replied the proprietor, 'but I'm afraid the basement is not open to the public.' The man went round to the magazine counter and looked at *Dance and Dancers, Dancing Times* and a few others and then came back and made a further attempt to descend the stairs. 'Are you sure I can't go downstairs?' he asked 'Not unless I push you down' was the somewhat brusque reply. The man had the sense to go; it looked as though the threat might have actually been carried out. Several customers present found this little sideshow hugely amusing. So, we will leave the basement and the famous spiral staircase for the time being and begin on a three year journey of delight.

CHAPTER TWO

At first we were 'Miss Trigg' and 'Mr Beaumont'. Those were not the days of instant Christian names and such titles would have been quite proper. But one day, after he had presented me to Alicia Markova, I said that I would rather like it if he would call me Isabelle. He was dubious; 'I've never called an assistant by her Christian name before', he said. I looked at him, perhaps a little pleadingly. 'But then,' he continued, 'I've never had an assistant like you before... All right then. Isabelle'. 'Dear Mr B,' I said, 'thank you'.

Markova was not, of course, the only famous person to visit the shop. At some time or other it seemed as if almost every dancer in the world must have visited 75 Charing Cross Road. For those in foreign companies it was often their first outing in London and they came not just to see the famous shop but to talk to the great Cyril Beaumont whose usually quiet demeanour concealed a first-class brain and a wealth of knowledge. Writer and translator of more than 100 books, ballet critic, printer, publisher, friend of the famous, as well as owning a shop full of wonderful books.

Letters would come afterwards, sometimes in another language, saying how much they had appreciated the visit and listening to 'The Master's' exposition on this or that aspect of ballet. I, too, got letters sometimes. One arrived addressed economically to 'Isabelle, Charing

Cross Road, London'. Mr B peered at this, back and front, before handing it over. 'Hmm' he said 'I don't like the look of this. People might begin to wonder about the nature of the place'.

Dancers from Sadler's Wells Ballet (as it then was) and from companies elsewhere in the world would come to him for enlightenment on a new role, or even an old one, and it was not unusual for them to say, after what had been virtually a master class on the interpretation of the role, that they had learnt more in half an hour from him than they had ever learnt from anyone else in weeks. To those who could not speak English his fluent French, which he had learnt from his mother and the family's French maid sufficed. Like Churchill, he felt that French should be relayed in an English accent. He spoke some Russian as well and once sent a message on a card to Nathalie Krassovska, then guest ballerina with Festival Ballet. When she read it in her dressing room she said, 'That ees not Russian – ees Polish'. 'Oh' said Mr B when I laughingly told him, 'I speak Polish and I didn't even know'.

After I had been at 75 for a few months I suggested that Mr B should keep a journal. Almost every day someone of note came into the shop, not only dancers but producers, authors, poets, actors... In and out they went, always adding something to the general diversity and (to me) excitement of working there. He would dictate to me and I would write down all the comings and goings of the day. Alas, there was seldom time to write more than a few sentences each day (and those I still have) and sometimes nothing at all. The project was soon abandoned and I announced my intention of writing my own journal. This idea filled Mr B with foreboding. 'Do mind what you write in it,' he said. 'There's a lot that goes on here which is not for the general public,' making it sound as if the place was a den of intrigue. It was true, many confidences were expressed there and several scandals exposed and nothing was ever kept from me; in fact I was quite often asked for an opinion. But I proceeded, writing as much as I had time for each day, often late into the night. Occasionally something would happen or be recounted there that really was not for general consumption or the Press and he would say with some alarm, 'For goodness' sake don't put *that* in your journal!' I continued to write it for several years and a copy of it is now in the Archives of the Royal Opera House.

Over the months I gathered a large group of acquaintances and friends who would come into the shop, often just to chat to me about the previous night's performance at the Garden, somebody's first performance, Fonteyn's dreaded retirement and a host of other topics. Mr B's reaction was, 'If we stopped selling books and all your friends paid half a crown each time they came in, we might make some money'. Many of the callers were young dancers, perhaps having just come from class in West Street, with little or no money to spend. I found a cardboard box and filled it with cuttings from old magazines and priced them all at one penny. These gave a legitimate excuse for a visit, and half an hour could be spent burrowing about in the box and chatting meanwhile to me, busy wrapping parcels to be taken to the Post Office.

One day a young man entered the shop and immediately engaged himself in conversation with me. He looked at some new publications, gave me a cheque to settle his monthly account (which was quite substantial) and told me he was a medical student at University College Hospital. He did prattle on rather but by then I was used to all sorts of customers and didn't pay too much heed. Finally the young man prepared to depart, saying that he would be back soon. I prayed that it would not be at a time when we were busy! Opening a door that led to the office, I found Mr B with a look of alarm on his face. 'Who was that bird out there?' he asked. I told him. 'Well', he said, 'he talks too much'. I pointed out that that 'bird' was one of our best account customers. No matter, he had a fear of my friendship (even acquaintance, sometimes) with any members of the male sex, feeling certain that their one intent was to whisk me off (to what or where I am not sure) and that he would lose me. 'You are very precious to me' he would say, which was touching and delightful but in the case of the young medical student, Michael Stoughton, his worst fears were confirmed because some years later I married him. I don't think Mr B ever forgave him. On our wedding day I received a handsome brass tray and my husband-to-be a statement for his monthly account.

A couple of days after I had arrived at 75, Mr B had mentioned to me that his wife was not very well. I expressed immediate sympathy and asked what ailed her. He said that she had broken a leg and had been walking on crutches which had caused arthritis in the other leg. Thinking this was perhaps a month or two beforehand I was amazed when, in answer to my question as to when this had occurred, he said '1939 in Bournemouth'. *Before the war* and this was 14 years later. 'Have you any children?' I asked, because I really wanted to know about him and his life outside the shop. 'No,' he said sadly. 'We never had time for that sort of thing. We were always too busy in the shop'. I found that answer ambiguous but kept my counsel about the interpretation I put on it.

Cyril Beaumont had married Alice Behar on 10th December 1914. He had, as one might say, 'inherited' her with the shop in 1910 and it was she who had guided him through all the ways of the bookseller's world. I think she might well have been a handsome woman at the time of the marriage, but by the time I knew her some 40 years later, her face bore the marks of pain and suffering and, frankly, of discontent. She kept a tight rein on her husband and liked him to be back at the flat in Bedford Court Mansions promptly at meal times. I remember her telephoning one day at about 5.30pm and demanding to know 'Where is Cyril? He should have been home half an hour ago. I've re-boiled the kettle three times and all the oxygen has gone out of the water.' Nevertheless, he was devoted to her and although there were many little outings and occurrences from time to time and I became used to the injunction 'Better not tell my wife', he always insisted that it was his duty to look after her because she had helped him so much when he first came to the shop.

She and I were on pleasant and friendly terms although, goodness knows, I must have done a number of things of which she did not quite approve and when Mr B made his annual visit to the Edinburgh Festival in August, I would go and visit her every day and keep her 'up to date' as she liked to call it. One year she felt so ill just before he was due to leave that he almost cancelled the visit, but realising that the train ticket, the hotel and seats in the theatre in Edinburgh were all booked, he decided at the last minute that he must go. I still have the letter that he wrote to me detailing the wonderful *Romeo and Juliet* performed by the Royal Danish Ballet and telling me also the dilemma the night before he left. 'But I relied on your loving kindness' he wrote, 'and knew that you would look after her'. That letter was written as was usual with a mapping pen with the lines so close together that it took me three quarters of an hour to decipher it. But the account of the Royal Danes' *Romeo and Juliet*, described in minute detail, was more than worth the effort. He had a visual memory and perfect recall, which was why so many dancers found his descriptions of old ballets and dancers so enthralling, because they all came to life so realistically. His many books on ballets, such as *The Ballet called Giselle, The Ballet called Swan Lake*, and the *Complete Book of Ballets* and many others are still in use today.

CHAPTER THREE

Cyril Beaumont's sense of humour was somewhat naïve and unsophisticated. He would tell his jokes with a desire to amuse, almost always adding the question, 'Don't you think that's funny?' One morning while taking off his hat and coat, he asked me, 'Which do you think is the happier: an infant in infancy or an adult in adultery?' There was a little chuckle and the day began well. Another time, there was the tale of the somewhat dim young lady who accompanied her gentleman friend to an important social gathering of the society of which he was a member. 'And this,' he said to her, moving towards an imposing elderly man, 'is the Vice-President, Mister So-and-So.' 'Oh,' gushed the young woman, 'so pleased to meet you. Which particular vice are you the president of?' More chuckles.

There were some little diversifications of pronunciation he used which might have sounded odd coming from others, but to me – and to many people – they were just part of the unique and endearing Beaumont personality. One example was an utterance that always came before the imparting of confidential information: 'This is strictly entre nous' he would say, but placing an acute accent at the end of 'entre', it became 'this is strictly entré nous'. The word 'interesting' was pronounced unfailingly as 'interESTing'; his annual visit to Scotland was always to the 'Edingborough Festival'. Telling me of the first night of a ballet (I forget which), he described the first act as consisting of 'permituitions' on a theme. Talking of one of the earliest known ballets he would speak of what sounded like 'The Female Guardee'.

A visitor complaining of a headache or not feeling quite well would be asked, 'Would you like a sniff of my bottle?' and from a waistcoat pocket would be withdrawn a little bottle of smelling salts, proffered across the desk. People usually agreed, whether they liked the smell or not, because it was one of his little courtesies. My grandmother and her sisters had had similar 'little bottles' but I had never before seen a man carry one. At the first symptoms of a cold or cough I would be advised to 'Go to bed with Vick.' It was a good job that I knew 'Vick' was a medicament sold in a little tin, the aroma from which would soothe a blocked nose or a tickling cough. 'I have to be careful with that advice', he said once with a little grin.

He himself once complained of a pain in his shoulder (the right, I think), grasping it with his opposite hand and giving an intake of breath. 'Is it arthritis?' I asked solicitously. 'No', he said, 'It's a legacy of being a pall-barer at Nijinsky's funeral. I would never have thought that the coffin would be so heavy'. Nijinsky's funeral? That was in 1950! Was he to have a permanent reminder of the event? But apart from the attacks of bronchitis every winter, Mr B seemed usually to enjoy good health; perhaps it was the walk from Bedford Court Avenue and back twice a day that kept him so. Mrs Beaumont, on the other hand, seemed thoroughly to enjoy bad health and was once very put out when a well-wisher at Covent Garden congratulated her, Mr B having told her that his wife was a 'little better'. 'Indeed I am not' retorted Alice smartly. 'Cyril has no idea of how I feel.' On the whole it seemed better when asked about his wife's health to say 'Not too well I'm afraid.' That dealt with everyone's feelings.

While being among the most generous givers himself Mr B was a man to whom it was almost impossible to give a present which suited him. Pleased at the thought behind the giving, it did not, however, take long before the gift began to reveal its drawbacks and general incompatibility with the recipient. Once for his birthday, I gave him a coat-hanger which (literally) doubled up as a clothes brush. I thought it very ingenious and hoped he might find it useful. It was clear, however, from the outset that the very idea of something masquerading as something else was not to his taste. Daily, it seemed, the thing became more recalcitrant and aggressive until one day it actually 'swung round and pinched me on the finger.' I took it away and I have it still. Neither of us could bear it any longer.

One day, at the end of the visit of the Paris Opéra Ballet in 1955, Nina Vyroubova had called at the shop after we had closed. She bore 'A little gift for M. Beaumont' and had taken it back to her hotel with instructions that it should be collected from there. He was not at all pleased that she should expect time to be wasted (my time, naturally) in collecting something which almost certainly he did not want. Unfortunately, dear Nina V. had given the name of her hotel incorrectly and I spent an entire afternoon chasing this wretched gift from one place to another until I finally located it and bore it back to 75 not in the best of tempers. Mr B undid the – by now – somewhat untidy parcel and revealed its contents. Why on earth had I bothered? Vyroubova's 'little gift' consisted of an amber-coloured plastic ball with holes bearing different coloured pencils. We looked at it in horror. 'God's truth!' he said in amazement. 'Why on earth did she give me that? It's not my sort of thing at all... I mean, I'm grateful for the thought but what on earth ARE they?' 'Pencils' I said weakly. 'Yes, but what are they FOR?' he persisted 'Writing?' I suggested. 'No' he replied, his eyes slightly glazed. 'Its more like makeup... Red for lipstick, blue for eyeshadow, black for mascara... I mean I'm very grateful for the thought, but why on earth did she give them to me? What can I do with them? They're not my sort of thing at all. I'm grateful for the thought...' It began to sound like a gramophone record. Every visitor who came into the office in the following week gazed in horrified disbelief at the garish and incongruous ornament on the great CWB's desk and was told the same story. 'Sending Isabelle over half London to collect that... it's not that I'm not grateful for the thought, but why on earth...?' In the end that too had to be removed. It was altogether too painful for either of us to endure any longer.

Yet, when it came to giving to others, he was always most thoughtful, trying hard to select what he thought would please the recipient. I was the fortunate receiver of a number of gifts, quite often his own books. Any dancer in hospital received flowers, fruit and cards of good wishes – I know, I delivered them. One day in his absence I sold a very expensive book to an unknown customer, who willingly paid the full price. On his return Mr B was delighted and selecting a copy of his little book 'Margot Fonteyn' he wrote in it 'For Isabelle, who is a great help to me in the conduct of business at 75 Charing Cross Road.'

At Christmas I would receive toiletries of one sort or another, he having ascertained by what he considered 'subtle means' the scents I liked. Sometimes there was very welcome extra money. A young Icelandic student at the Royal Academy of Music was given a carefully-chosen hand-sewn leather music case which she herself could never have afforded. She was one of Mr B's 'young ladies', of whom there were several, and while I am absolutely certain that there was nothing remotely improper about these friendships, they were mostly of the 'Better not tell my wife' sort. I think that they stemmed from the fact that he had no children of his own and he saw something of compelling interest in youth, with all its possibilities.

Among those most dear to him was Svetlana Beriosova, newly promoted from Sadler's Wells Theatre Ballet to the main company. She regarded him with admiration and awe and when she was given her first major classical role in 1954 (Aurora in *Sleeping Beauty*), she came to Mr B in fear and trembling to learn from him something of the role when danced by what she called 'The great ones'. He simply talked to her, no histrionics, no demonstrations (he had, after all, never been a dancer) but just quiet explanations of the different parts of Aurora's role. He had, it must be remembered, been at the very first English production in 1921. I had, at some point, said to Mr B how wrong it looked, how out of character for the Princess to *throw* the roses at her mother during the Rose Adage. Surely she, as a loving and deferential daughter, would have *taken* the flowers and presented them to the Queen. Mr B thought this over and pronounced complete agreement. He passed the suggestion on to Svetlana who loved it and, to my delight and his approval, incorporated it into the part.

During one of her several visits prior to the first night of her *Beauty* (1 June 1954) Mr B thought of a photograph that might be of help. It was held in the basement's brown paper parcel filing system and he knew exactly where to look. As he descended the stairs Svetlana and I turned to each other and said simultaneously 'Isn't he wonderful'. I wondered what I should give her as a first night gift. Mr B, once more visiting his treasure-house in the basement, brought up an old souvenir programme in which was a picture of Olga Spessivtseva as Aurora. Dear Roy Round, my good and helpful photographer friend, made a copy of the picture and then printed it with remarkably good effect. I had it mounted on a pink background and on the day attached pink roses to it. 'Mr B', It says in my journal for 31 May, 'very sweetly helped me with the mount. He is as pleased with the result as I am'. His own first night present to her was a white china snail which he had searched for and found somewhere. I filled it for him with forget-me-nots and one cyclamen-coloured rose and then placed it in a box lined with pink tissue paper and covered the whole with cellophane. We were both in a state of excitement for her and I was almost as nervous as she was. Months afterwards, Svetlana told me that she kept the picture I had given her in her bedroom and took it with her whenever she went away.

Some time later an invitation to take Sunday tea at 68 Bedford Court Mansions was issued by Mrs B to Svetlana who accepted with pleasure. But, on hearing that I should not be there also, she was disappointed and became slightly apprehensive. 'Mrs Beaumont frightens me a bit,' she said. I could see why, but in the event I think the time was pleasantly spent.

Many famous people came into the shop either to look at new books or just to talk to Mr B. Some he had known since the Diaghilev days, others because they were authors, or dancers of the present time. If the shop should be empty of people for 15 minutes, one would wonder if Charing Cross Road had been closed or there had been a small earthquake outside the shop. It was not long before I knew everyone who came there, Mr B always presented me to them. 'I do so' he said, 'so that you will always be able to say you've met them'. One day we had a visit from Lydia Lopokova wearing a hat so large and so covered in strange ornamentation that it overshadowed her tiny form. She puffed away at a cigarette all the time she was talking, he meanwhile sending me agonised glances at the sight. He hated people smoking in the shop and would say at their departure, 'Thank God he's gone, before he burnt the shop down'. He and the great Lopokova chatted about the most ordinary matters it seemed to me, and suddenly she said to us both, 'What do you think of my hat? Isn't it wonderful? I bought it in Cambridge for £3-10s'. Upon her departure he gave the usual sigh of relief about going before the shop was burnt down, then added, 'And as for the hat – more like 3/6d in a jumble sale.' So was one of Diaghilev's most famous dancers, wife of one of the most famous men in England (Maynard Keynes) dismissed.

CHAPTER FOUR

On the 30 December 1954, George Goncharov – beloved teacher of so many dancers for years – died of cancer of the liver. He had suffered for so long before consulting a doctor that, when he finally did so, nothing could be done. It threw the ballet world into terrible sadness and it seemed that people could talk of nothing else. I had got to know him and love him dearly over many months; he was that sort of man. Just before 11 o'clock on the morning of 4 January, Mr B and I made our way through a blizzard to St Martin-in-the-Fields for the funeral. It was like walking onto the set in a theatre: the white coffin covered in white lilac and pink chrysanthemums and music from *Swan Lake* coming from the organ. I sat with Mr B on one side and Margot Fonteyn on the other, she weeping silently into her handkerchief. Later, when the coffin was borne away and music from the last act of *Swan Lake* was being played, Margot cried bitterly, remembering perhaps 25 years ago when she was a little girl in Shanghai and Goncharov was her teacher.

As the people left, Canon Mortlock, the priest who had conducted the service, came to the pew where we sat and Margot thanked him for the moving eulogy he had given. 'Everything you said about him was so true,' she said. 'You must have known him very well.' 'I did not know him at all,' said Canon Mortlock, 'But it was all so true,' she said, 'I felt sure you had known him.' 'Ah,' said the

Canon with a smile, 'that was Divine inspiration guiding me.' He did not mention that Mr B had spent a long time on the preceding Saturday telling him all that he knew of George Goncharov.

****

I often heard amusing stories of Mr B's early days as a bookseller. His father had bought the shop in 1910 and given it to his son in the hope that he would make a career for himself as a bookseller. The young Cyril knew nothing of business and thought that the chequebook with which his father had presented him a very good idea. It was an unpleasant surprise when he realised that cheques were no good without money in the bank. A man once asked the fledgling bookseller for a book on 'China' and after he had climbed to the top of the stepladder and brought down a large volume on China and Tibet, the man threw it at him and said angrily, 'Not that you fool – I want a book on porcelain.'

One could say there was never a dull moment at 75 Charing Cross Road. In the intervals between customers, when he was not busy writing *The Sunday Times* article or working on his next book, I would be regaled with such stories as the foregoing one, and many of them concerned the Diaghilev days. He had known Diaghilev well and was privy to rehearsals, performances, backstage and many incidents outside the theatre. There was the story of the dinner party given by the great man where among the guests (including CWB) was Sacheverell Sitwell, at that time in the army and stationed at Aldershot. Pressed by Diaghilev several times to stay on at the

feast, Sitwell had replied that he could not do so as he had
to get back to Aldershot. 'Qui est cette 'Aldershot'?' de-
manded his host 'Est-ce-que le nom de votre maîtresse?'
The remembrance of this event still made Mr B chuckle
and was accompanied by the inevitable 'Don't you think
that's funny?'

There were tales of how he and the newly-wed Alice
had kept the shop open from 10am until 8pm but were
actually there long before and long after opening and
closing time. He told me with some relish of a nearby food
shop where, if you arrived with your own plate, you received a fair helping of boiled beef and carrots for 6d. A
small gas cooker had been installed in the basement on
which could be cooked simple meals and tea made. It
seemed that they were often on the premises until after
10pm. I began to see why there were no children.

There was always a wealth of correspondence arriving
at the shop, most of which had to be answered. Asked one
day by a visiting dancer with some awe, 'Do you answer
all these letters yourself, Mr Beaumont?' He replied 'Well,
no; Isabelle and I do them between us.' I realised then that
I had become a fixture there and was delighted by the
fact.

CHAPTER FIVE

Perhaps now is the time to write the story of 'The Firebird Fracas' referred to in chapter one. This episode revealed another dimension of Mr B's character which is of greater importance: that of his formidable memory, not only of events but of every detail of those events. It also reveals his tenacity and determination to prove the truth and a degree of intellectual superiority that dwarfed his opponents.

A new production of Fokine's *The Firebird (l'Oiseau de Feu)* by Serge Grigoriev and Lubov Tchernicheva was given by Sadler's Wells Ballet at the Edinburgh Festival on 9 August 1954. Mr B wrote me a long and – as usual – tightly written letter describing the first night. He did not like the production – 'I do not care much for it as a choreographic work. It seems very dated,' he wrote. He was thinking back to the original Golovin setting. 'I shall not be popular,' he said. And that was just the beginning of 'The Firebird Fracas'.

On his return to London he enlarged his description of the first night. 'It was all so hard,' he said. 'Fonteyn rendered the Firebird as a bird of prey when in fact she was a frightened, captive bird, pleading with Ivan Tsarevitch to release her and offering him a feather in exchange for her release.' I found all this most difficult to comprehend. After all, Fonteyn had been coached in the role by Tamara Karsavina who was the original Firebird and who, in turn, must have been told by Fokine what sort of bird she was supposed to be.

The first night came at the Royal Opera House on 31 August and I was utterly enchanted. Maybe, as Mr B said, (and he was there at both productions) it was not as splendid and wonderful as the original, but to me, and to most people there, it was something of supreme beauty and a great experience. He, however, had to write as he knew it to be and as it had been. Again, he said that Fonteyn danced brilliantly but in Frederick Ashton's style rather than in Fokine's simpler, more tender manner.

Not only did war break out in *The Sunday Times'* letters column, but with visitors to the shop (a number of whom remembered the original) and even in the coffee house in Soho where I had lunch every day and so did many people connected with the theatre and the press in some way. I began to feel very sorry for poor Margot – torn in two directions, in one way by Karsavina, the original Firebird and in the other by Cyril Beaumont, an acknowledged authority on ballet both as a critic and an historian, and for whom she had great regard and respect.

Most vociferous in their opinions of Mr B's review of the first night were Anton Dolin and Keith Lester (who at that time was choreographer at the Windmill Theatre). Their letters became strident and overbearing, quite vicious in fact, claiming that of course dancers must know more about the subject than 'a critic who saw a few performances of the ballet'. The Editor later told Mr B that Dolin's letter had been couched in its entirety in such very rude terms that he had censored it.

Various people, including many visitors to 75, began to question the soundness of Karsavina's memory; after all, it was more than forty years since she had danced the role. Could time have clouded her remembrance? She declared that the Firebird was a bird of prey. Cyril Beaumont said the Firebird was a captive bird. He showed me a book, very old and in Russian, with a picture of four ballerinas in the role of Firebird. The one of Karsarvina with Adolph Bolm showed the latter as the Tsarevitch seizing the Firebird by the wrists and her eyes are full of terror and pleading. She was certainly no bird of prey when that was taken.

I remembered how, not long ago, one of Kathleen Crofton's pupils bought a postcard from Mr B of Karsavina taken in about 1911. She took it to Karsavina's mime-class and asked her to autograph it. 'Who is it?' asked Karsavina 'It is you, Madam' said the child. 'Me? Good Heavens!' The girl then asked her in which ballet she appeared in the photograph, to which Karsavina replied that she hadn't the faintest idea. So back it came to Mr B who knew immediately that it was one of the ballet sequences from Delibes' opera 'Lakmé.

One evening during the Interval at Covent Garden, 'Mim' Rambert made her way to Mr B to tell him that it was 'a revelation' to her that the Firebird was a bird of prey, and she had been a member of Diaghilev's Company. Alicia Markova, out front one night, told Mr B that the interpretation was nothing like the one she remembered.

Ram Gopal came in one day and immediately plunged into the *Firebird* affair. (It seemed that no one in half of London talked of anything else). He said that he had been to have tea with Karsavina and had tried to talk to her about Nijinsky. He said that her recollections seemed vague and when he asked her to describe Nijinsky's elevation, which had been phenomenal (and he and Karsavina had worked closely together in Diaghilev's Company), Gopal had received the distinct impression that her memory was failing because his question prompted no response at all for some time. Then, at last, she said, 'Elevation? Yes, it was very big.'

Karsavina herself wrote to *The Sunday Times* regarding CWB's article after the first night of *Firebird*, saying how thoroughly she disagreed with him, and if anyone should know, she should, having been the first Firebird. Mr B replied in a letter which was masterly although unfortunately I do not have a copy of it. But Fonteyn's performance was altering: she seemed to have hardened her interpretation and become a wild and angry bird rather than a timid creature trying to escape. Poor Margot – how bewildering this must all have been for her. It was somewhat bewildering for me, caught up as I was in the maelstrom of bird of prey and captive bird. Even if Karsavina had forgotten, I thought, how could Grigoriev, not to mention Tchernicheva have forgotten as well? It seemed to me quite fantastic that Karsavina should say that Fonteyn's interpretation resembled her own if it didn't. To me, Fonteyn's performance was utterly wonderful but then I had seen no other. Mr B said that if I had seen the Diaghilev production I would see more of the weaknesses of this one. I didn't know whether to feel sorry for myself that I hadn't seen it, or sorry for him that he had because it had obviously spoiled his enjoyment of the present one. My journal entry sometime in November 1954 describes 'Fonteyn's astounding bird-like movements, now like a streak of fire crossing the stage, now heartbreaking in her endeavours to escape captivity'.

On the morning of 4 January, the day of poor Goncharov's funeral, I met Ninette de Valois on the tube. She pounced upon me and went straight into the subject of *Firebird*. She said without hesitation that OF COURSE Mr Beaumont was wrong and Karsavina was right. I asked her how she reconciled a bird of prey with Ivan's capturing it with his bare hands but she brushed this aside with, 'Oh my dear, it's a *fairy story*'. I told her that many people who saw the original production had written to Mr B and came into the shop daily and agreed with him, but she got over that by saying that however clever a critic might be and however many years he had been going to the ballet, his approach was not that of a dancer and there must always remain a gap between the layman's and the professional's outlook. I was not at all convinced because I felt that she was only stating what she wanted to be the case and not what was the truth. We almost got carried on to the next station in the heat of the argument. 'You tell that boss of yours...' she said as we squeezed through the closing doors at Leicester Square. I did tell 'that boss of mine', in detail. 'Just think' I said, 'I argued with the great de Valois'. 'Well' he said, 'I think you should feel quite flattered that she did argue with you'. Anyway, she could have been in no doubt about whose side I was on.

I knew that CWB was not going to give up this battle; it had become war to the knife and he was going to win. Although his exterior was calm and courteous I knew that inside his blood was stirred. So! The time had come for recourse to the brown paper parcel filing system. With the by now familiar ESP movements of the hands the required parcel was extracted from the rack and opened. I watched with admiration and amazement as he searched through a pile of seemingly random press cuttings. He knew exactly that for which he was looking and after some minutes there came a triumphant 'Here it is!'

'It' was a a press cutting with the post script to the original letter which had been omitted the previous week for 'reasons of space'. It was printed in the following week as a post script to the Lester and Dolin letters and read: 'As to the Folklorist conception of a Firebird, the latest Russian Encyclopaedia: Jar-Pitsa (Firebird) – an image encountered in Slavonic and particularly Russian fairy tales, a bird of incredible beauty with sparkling feathers. Obtained as a result of immense effort by the hero of a fairy tale, since it ensures future success. The image of the Firebird incarnates the people's yearning for happiness. (*Bolshaya Sovietskaya Encyclopaedia* in progress) Vol. 15 1952 p.599.

In Ershov's 'Koniok Gorbunok' (that is Humpbacked Horse) Ivanushka tries to catch a Firebird, the bait is a mixture of wine and oats.

In Zhukovsky's 'Tale of Ivan Tsaravitch and the Grey Wolf' the Firebird's food is apples which she steals from a tree (*Polnoe Sobranie Sochenenii* – Complete Works St Petersburg 1902).

I submit that none of the above conceptions suggests a bird of prey.'

The Sunday Times Editor, bless his heart, printed the findings in full, at the end of the two childishly rude letters from Lester and Dolin. Cyril Beaumont was, after all, a scholar, not just a retired dancer.

In *The Sunday Times* of 16 January 1955 there appeared Mr B's reply to the letters of Lester and Dolin. As happened quite often, he asked for my help, not with factual knowledge obviously, but in finding a suitable word or assembling a sentence to best advantage. 'Two heads are better than one.'
The letter was a masterpiece of understated annihilation. I submit it in full.

Sir, since neither Mr Dolin nor Mr Lester saw Mme Karsavina's interpretation at Covent Garden in 1912 – as I did on several occasions – they have no valid evidence to offer on the point at issue.

A former dancer who worked under Fokine has written to me: 'Fonteyn's actual movements are the same as Karsavina's but the interpretation and feeling are very different.' That is my contention.

Mr Dolin concedes that *The Firebird is* a fairy tale – but not a beneficent one. Yet the Firebird saves Ivan from being turned to stone by Kostchei.

Mr Lester's account of Spessivtseva's rendering of the role is interesting, but we are concerned with Madam Karsavina's interpretation. It may be that the dynamics of movement can only be fully grasped by dancers, but how many audiences are composed entirely of dancers? In any case, one does not need to be a dancer to distinguish between a savage bird of prey or the reverse.

Cyril Beaumont

The *coup de grace* came when the Editor produced a footnote.
'After the first performance in England of *Firebird* our

ballet critic of the day wrote in *The Sunday Times* of June
23 1912: 'Mme Karsovina (sic) took the name-part and
quite unforgettable was her birdlike grace and fleetness of
movement and the suggestion of palpitating fear and vio-
lated purity with which she shrank from the arms of her
captor'.

The Editor regrets that this correspondence must now
be closed.

And that was the end of '*The Firebird* Fracas'.

Fonteyn's Firebird began to change. Not drastically or
dramatically but by small differences in her interpretation. She became the captured bird, but a bird with power.
Gradually a little pathos crept in, as she offered Ivan the
feather, pleading with him to let her go. I was delighted
with all this. I felt it meant that she had thought over Mr
B's words as to what sort of bird 'l'Oiseau' was. She was
now giving a lyrical performance. Ashton, too, had altered his Kostchei, which became a much stronger
character (Mr B had had a 'little talk' with him just before
Christmas). He altered his wig and beard so they look less
like those of 'a demented scarecrow' (I wrote in my journal) and was much more frightening than he had been in
earlier performances.

Altogether, the result of so much *sturm und drang* was a
damning and positive victory for Cyril Beaumont whose
quiet, painstaking scholarship overwhelmed the
mannerless discourtesy from those who had dismissed
him as 'just a critic'.

I learned much from it.

CHAPTER SIX

The gas-fire in 'The Small Back Room' of 75 Charing Cross Road was, as I have previously indicated, the bane of my life. It was small and consisted of about five crumbling bars which looked like decaying teeth. It was temperamental as to whether or not it should be lit, sometimes not responding to the proffered match and at other times lighting only after a resounding 'pop!' By today's standards of 'health and safety' it would have been condemned long ago, along with the staircase and a good many other things. Even when lit, the flickering blue and yellow flames gave out little heat and as it was the only form of heating in the entire establishment, I often froze in the winter. Nevertheless, Mr B and the wretched apparatus had a constant battle. If I lit it on a cold morning, he would, after a short time, pronounce the atmosphere 'very stuffy' and I would be advised to turn it down. On what I might consider quite a warm day he would say that he felt cold and 'better light the fire'. The one wretched sash window looking out at bricks and mortar only a few feet away seemed to go hand in hand with the gas-fire to see which could bother the proprietor most. 'It's chilly in here,' he would say, on a stifling summer's day, 'better shut the window'. Sometimes I would open the shop door in order not to die of suffocation but before long the noise from the Charing Cross Road traffic became unbearable and a plaintive cry would come from behind the magisterial desk to 'shut the door or I shall go deaf'. The accompanying actions were dramatic: the heat of the fire would force him to mop his brow with his handkerchief and the noise of the traffic force him to put his hands over his ears. There was, as one might say, never a dull moment.

****

As well as the big, important things for which Cyril Beaumont was most well known, there was an infinite number of small things which had, in their own way, just as much influence on the life of the many dancers who crossed his path.

Some time in June of 1954 Nadia Nerina rang to talk to me about a book containing the choreography of *The Dying Swan* which we were trying to get for her. She intended to take this (*The Dying Swan*) to South Africa and was taking lessons from Cleo Nordi, who had been in Pavlova's Company. She asked if I could find out from Mr B the size of the jewel worn by Pavlova on her costume. She had seen several pictures of this but the costume of Pavlova's seen in the South Kensington Museum seemed smaller. I talked to Mr B about this and he asked her to come in and he would bring a jewel in to show her. It was large and of a glorious blue, surrounded by rhinestones. There were, in fact, several costumes for *The Dying Swan* and each had a different stone, some red, some blue and were of differing sizes. Who else, I wonder, knew that?

My friend Sonya Hana, later to marry Peter Wright who became the first Director of Birmingham Royal Ballet, was appearing in *The King and I* at Drury Lane during the 1950s. One day in July 1955 she and I had tea together, as in fact we did every week after the matinee on Wednesday. She said that Kathleen Crofton had asked her to appear as guest-artist in a Sunday Concert at the Royal Court Theatre in September. Sonya had agreed because the solo, by Rupert Doone, was in the Japanese style (Sonya was half-Japanese) but was worried because he had told her 'It is a little like *Mme Chrysanthème* but I thought of this long before Ashton did'. That phrase rang the alarm bell. I asked her to demonstrate some of the steps and movements involved which she did on the floor of her dressing room. The whole thing bore such a remarkable resemblance to Fifield's solo in *Chrysanthème* – even to the fans used – that I felt quite startled. My advice to her was not to do it because I felt that it would reflect badly on her, personally, to do something which was such obvious plagiarism. So she rang Crofton the next day and got herself out of it. I told all this to Mr B and asked if he thought my advice to Sonya had been right. He said that he thought it had, because although Rupert Doone choreographed a ballet called *The Enchanted Grove* for the Vic-Wells in 1932 which was certainly in the Japanese-cum-classical style, people didn't generally remember it. On the other hand, *Mme Chrysanthème* was fresh in everybody's mind and the obvious inference would be that the new Doone had been plagiarised from the latter. Once more, who else in the whole of London, or the whole of the ballet world, would have known that?

One Thursday in April of 1956 while having lunch with Rowena Jackson, who had become a good friend, she told me that she had found herself down to do Myrtha

(Queen of the Wilis in *Giselle*) the following Saturday and she knew absolutely nothing about the role. Not unnaturally she was fearful, wondering how she could possibly get to grips with the part in less in two days. I asked Mr B if he would see her and go through the role with her. She told me afterwards that he had helped her more in half an hour than anybody in the Sadler's Wells Ballet could have done in a week. As a result she gave a really splendid interpretation, very strong and evil, and looking exactly like a corpse drawn up from the grave to weave magic spells on the living. At his suggestion she had smeared Vaseline on her cheeks to give a look of putrefaction. I was very pleased with her and so was Mr B. I think she was quite pleased with herself too, although a little apprehensive in case she had not done what he meant. But she said it had felt right and she was exhausted.

****

When Festival Ballet produced *Esmeralda* in July 1954, Natalie Krassovska (Tata) who was to play the name-role, came into the shop to talk to Mr B about her hair, which she could not decide how to dress for the first night. He showed her various pictures of former Esmeraldas and she was delighted at the suggestion of two small pigtails or bunches. There was, quite simply, in the whole of London, no one else who could have helped her. It was not only that his advice to dancers was practical, it also gave them peace of mind which was very important.

****

When I first began working at 75 Charing Cross Road, I would arrive at 10am, when the shop opened, and Mr B would be there already. After a week or two this changed and I was the one to open up the shop and Mr B would arrive at 10.30 which, he said, 'suited' him. After about a week of my being there, I arrived one day and went into the office. Mr B rose from his seat, placed his hands on my shoulders and said, 'I shall now kiss you in the French manner' I was slightly alarmed until I received a peck on each cheek and was released. This chaste embrace continued every day that I worked there and I rather liked it.

It was a greeting given to all comers to the shop for whom he felt affection and included many dancers. Perhaps his favourite among these was Svetlana Beriosova, whom he loved dearly and who was devoted to him. She sought his wise counsel before every new role and would often say to me after the first night 'Do please tell Mr Beaumont I did everything he said'. He dedicated *Ballets Past and Present* to her in 1955 and I was sworn to secrecy until the day of publication. This was difficult since she and I were the dearest of friends and saw a great deal of each other. However, I managed it, and she was overjoyed when finally all was revealed.

Another favourite visitor was a little girl called Alexandra Kirsta, the daughter of George Kirsta who founded Ballet Comique. Mr B was extremely fond of Alexandra and took a great interest in her ability to write, to dance and to speak in advance, one might say, of her years. He often talked about her when she was not there, referring to her as 'Little Choura' (the Russian diminutive of Alexandra). Just after her 11th birthday she came to the shop and announced her intention of writing her 'life story'. What did Mr Beaumont think? He, I recorded in my journal, encouraged her to 'start writing about your ballet life, since you have the ability to write and something to write about'. She was later a bridesmaid at my wedding and is still my dear friend. Now herself a successful writer it was she who urged me to write this book.

One afternoon, soon after the to-do about *Firebird*, I was alone in the shop, Mr B having departed on one of his frequent trips to the Reading Room at the British Museum. These visits were mostly of a research nature (resulting one night in his getting locked in) but occasionally they were, I knew, a euphemism for some other activity in which case, he would say: 'If my wife rings I've gone to the Reading Room', and I asked no questions. Suddenly the shop door began to open in an uncertain sort of way as if the visitor were not quite sure of his welcome, and in sidled Anton Dolin. He looked, I thought, distinctively furtive. 'Good afternoon Mr Dolin' I said, determined to be business-like and not forthcoming in the usual way 'What can I do for you?' There was a slightly embarrassed pause, and then 'Er – I wondered if I could see Cyril for a moment or two', 'I'm sorry', I said 'Mr Beaumont is out on business. Do you wish to leave a message?' 'No, no', he said. 'Just tell him I came, I'll call later'. He seized the handle of the door, which actually he had never quite let go of, and made as if to retreat hastily. As he was half way out I called 'Shall I tell him you called to apologise?' There was not, of course, a reply. When Mr B came back and I told him the tale he was delighted at my parting shot and said that if he himself had been there

Dolin would have got something even sterner. *Firebird* had left its sores.

Some days later the wretched man did call again, this time obviously armed against any lack of enthusiasm on the part of the occupants of 75. It transpired that someone had left a book which they wanted him to sign, although why they should think he would be there to sign it I cannot imagine. Anyway, considering all things, including several less-than-enthusiastic reviews by Mr B of Festival Ballet (of which Dolin was Director) he was surprisingly cordial to us both, perhaps on the basis of 'if you can't beat them, join them'. Both Mr B and I contained ourselves honourably and were polite but decidedly cool towards him. Once again his exit was swift.

Every year towards the end of November, Mr B and I would sit down with a pile of Christmas cards and a list of future recipients and their addresses. It was really hard work; not only did he send somewhere in the region of 300 cards but all other work and people coming into the shop had to be accommodated. All the time we were ploughing our way through the rather dull job, Mr B would think of little anecdotes or descriptions of cartoons he had seen to tell me, always finishing with 'I think that's rather good, don't you?' He found humour in things which were quite often simple or even childish. But such was his way of repeating them that that in itself became amusing and we really enjoyed our Christmas card session. Dolin and Keith Lester were both struck off the list as, he stated, he was 'displeased' with them. That may seem droll now but was hardly surprising at the time since their behaviour over *Firebird* had been appalling and still rankled. Serge Lifar was also struck off in 1955, not for causing 'displeasure' but because 'He never sends me one, the wretch'. Walter Gore's name was also removed for failing to pay some money he owed. The familiar phrase 'I can get very nasty when I like' was brought into use.

One day just before Christmas, there arrived the most splendid and elaborate card. Inside it bore the charming inscription: 'To my dear Cyril and Mrs Beaumont, with many fond good wishes, Pat'. Mr B thought it was from Pat Hardy (quite who that was I do not now remember) but I recognised the handwriting as Dolin's. 'Good Lord', he said, 'So it is, the old wretch. Well he's not getting a card from me. I don't forget these things as easily as that', and Dolin's name stayed off the list.

Christmas cards were by mid December arriving in dozens both at the shop and at 68 Bedford Court Mansions. They were never displayed, there being no room at the shop and because at home Alice B did not apparently like the way they fell down when a door was opened. When I thought of the encumbered state of that flat I could not imagine that there would be a square inch anywhere to place a Christmas card. Everywhere was piled high with books, pictures, manuscripts, prints, letters, boxes, notes and general household impedimenta. The sideboard alone was stacked with bottles of fine wine including many of Champagne. 'Dear Mr B' I said 'Why on earth don't you drink some of this lovely wine?' 'Well' he said 'there's not time really' (what could that mean?) 'And what about all these bottles of Champagne?' Again 'Well,' with the head on one side, 'we've been waiting for something to celebrate.' Good grief , I thought... Some of the champagne was over 20 years old. Nothing to celebrate in 20 years? And if there ever should be, would the stuff be still worth drinking? Just one example of the Beaumont parsimony.

CHAPTER SEVEN

No recollection, no account, no description at life at 75 Charing Cross Road would be complete without mention of Montie Morris. William Beaumont Morris (unrelated to the owner of 75) known to all as Montie was, and had been for years, a frequent visitor to the shop, both as a customer and an occasional helper when needed and there was a degree of respect and friendship between the two men. In spite of this and the fact that they had known each other for years, they were 'Mr Beaumont' and 'Mr Morris' to each other. Montie and I soon became good friends, having, amongst other things, a similar sense of humour. Montie was what my mother used to describe as 'Not a marrying man'. His dress was somewhat descriptive of that; he always wore a bow-tie, a tightly-belted raincoat and a navy blue beret pulled somewhat rakishly over the right ear. He confided in me one day that although he and Mr B had known each other for years 'Yet he still calls me Mr Morris. You'd think he'd let up a bit by now, dear, wouldn't you?' It obviously made him quite sad. I had a little 'word' with Mr B. I said 'Poor Montie's quite sad that after such a long friendship you still call him Mr Morris.' 'Well,' he said, 'you know how I am, I don't use Christian names very much. I couldn't change now.' 'You call me by my Christian name,' I said. 'But you were very persuasive' he answered 'I've never done that before.' I fought on for dear Montie and at last Mr B gave me a defeated look and said 'We'll see how it goes.'

Two days later in walked WBM – glided actually would be a better description of how he moved. 'Good morning Mr Beaumont' he called through from the shop to the office. Mr B rose and came through the door, holding his hand out. I held my breath; 'Good morning Montie' he said, and 'Montie' he was ever afterwards.

'How'd you do it, dear?' he asked me when we were alone. 'Half a lifetime he's called me Mr Morris – this'll take some getting used to.'

Montie was a collector and an assembler. He would visit all the street markets of London (and Paris too, where he went every year) picking up antiquarian books on the ballet and theatre and using them as 'breakers', that is, he would cut out the often rare and exquisite pictures of dancers or theatre sets, then mount them and frame them. He called himself 'A scissors-and-paste Diaghilev'. He collected other things too, china, objets d'art and so on, but to a lesser degree. He could sometimes assist Mr B with some little-known photograph or print for use in a book and was himself extremely knowledgeable about the history of theatre.

He and I got on famously and in fact remained good friends for many years. One day he came to the shop when Mr B was out and announced his intention of examining one of the many packets of tea which had found rest in the basement since the war. 'It's wicked dear' he said, 'all that stuff down there going to waste'. It was he, in fact, who made the discovery that the tea in the packet he broke open was covered in mildew. As he climbed the

Montie Morris, aged 85, outside his lodgings in South Hampstead.

spiral staircase I could hear mutterings of: 'Wicked, absolutely wicked'.

'Oh Montie,' I said, 'what have you done? You've spilt tea all over the floor and we'll have to get rid of it.'

'I think we ought to tell him, dear' he said. 'Tell him all the tea is mouldy and there'll be rats down there soon.' But I deemed it best to let well alone. Knowledge of about half-a-hundredweight of mouldy tea in the basement would only cause Mr B to worry, because then he would feel that he ought to do something about it, and that could not be done without 'asking my wife'. So in the end it was agreed between us that we would say nothing, although Montie could not help a final: 'Wicked dear, all that food!'

We became the best of friends and remained so long after I was married. His excitement when I produced a son was immense: 'A dear little boo-boo' he said on first seeing him. When a second one appeared two years later, his joy knew no bounds. For some years Montie would come and spend Christmas at our house in Thames Ditton, staying for several days and spending time with my parents who lived nearby. For such visits his bow-tie would extend to something much grander, wider and of more exotic material. He and my father talked extensively about cricket – for some reason Montie found it a fascinating subject and knew a great deal of its history. They would sometimes meet and have lunch together in London. My mother found him fascinating, in spite of, or perhaps because of his 'not being a marrying man'.

Presents for all the family were beautiful and unique. I still have many of them – exotic pictures of dancers of the past, fashion plates, beautifully mounted and framed, and pieces of old china, bowls, plates and the like. I also have a folder full of letters from Montie, some hand written but mostly appallingly typed and with such idiosyncratic spelling that in their way they were just as difficult to read as Mr B's (not quite – nothing could ever be as obscure as those).

He was a dear friend to whom 'every day is a bonus' and when I heard that he had died at the age of 87 I wept. In his 'will' (which was no more than a collection of envelopes with the recipient's name on the outside and the name of the gift inside and half of which, when opened by his landlady, Lallie, were empty) he left me four long-stemmed Bohemian wine glasses, bright blue and richly engraved and a framed picture of Pavlova as 'The Dying Swan'. So I am reminded of him every day.

CHAPTER EIGHT

From time to time, perhaps every three months or so, we would have a visit from a tiny elderly lady called Miss Margaret Rolfe. She would suddenly dart into the shop – one saw her elaborate hat before her face appeared – and say that she had brought something for Mr Beaumont that would 'amuse him'. Miss Rolfe, by then well into her ninth decade, had as a child attended dancing classes given by Marie Taglioni at a salon in London. Her fellow pupil had been Princess May of Teck, later to become Queen Mary, wife of King George V. She and Mr B would chat about whatever came into the lady's head, and sometimes very strange things came into it. One day she looked at a photograph of a dancer (I have forgotten which one, fortunately) on the cover of the latest *Dancing Times*. 'Is that a serpent?' she asked, 'No' said Mr B, 'that is...' 'Well' said the lady, 'I am convinced that that is a serpent.' Occasionally she would remember small anecdotes concerning Taglioni but by far the greatest blessing of her visits was that she almost always brought some little trinket which had been given her by the great dancer herself, who must have taken a considerable interest in the little girl who was her pupil. I cannot remember most of them, although I believe there were some tiny gloves and there was certainly a fan. The fan was beautiful, white silk on one side and red satin on the other, in an ivory frame.

One evening towards the end of August 1955 when Mr B was in Edinburgh, I was preparing myself, as I always did, in the limited facilities of 75 for a visit to Covent Garden. I remembered how unbearably hot the theatre had been the night before and (I suppose rather wickedly) 'borrowed' the fan from the drawer where her treasures were tucked away and took it with me. I believe I must have been the first person to use it since Taglioni herself for I do not think Miss Rolfe ever used any of her bequests. It was an absolutely thrilling sensation actually to use it, which I did to good effect during the intense heat, but perhaps a little sacrilegious and I am not sure that Mr B would have approved. For me, though, it was one of the highlights of my ballet-going career.

Another slightly dubious action of mine (although not quite so bad as the fan, since it didn't leave the premises) was to put on my makeup whilst using a little hand-mirror which had belonged to Pavlova. This too was hidden in a drawer. It was round and quite small, framed and backed with ivory. The glass had a curious greenish tinge to it which had the advantage of making me think I looked rather more beautiful than in fact I was. Anyway, it was good for my morale after a hard day's work! In all probability Mr B would not have minded at all but I thought 'what the eye doesn't see the heart doesn't grieve over' and went happily off to meet whomever I was to drink iced coffee with in the Stalls Circle bar.

What with the last two misdemeanours and the 'borrowed' half-crown admitted to earlier, my list of crimes was growing.

****

One morning Mr B, methodically opening a stack of letters most of which he dismissed and put in the pile 'to be dealt with later', found one which was a charming letter from Yvette Chauviré which pleased him. Then the parcel post arrived and consisted of a copy of Lido's *Ballet 4* and Boris Kochno's *Le Ballet*, each autographed by its author. All these made him very happy and he sat behind his desk looking as pleased as a child at Christmas as he undid and admired his presents.

'And the next!' he called. 'No more,' I said 'that's quite enough for one morning.' He cried: 'What, no more? I was just beginning to enjoy myself!'

Some time later, knowing that I was going to see Fonteyn in *Giselle* that evening, he asked me to take a young Brazilian dancer to meet her. He had written a letter of introduction but Margot (who by this time knew me well) took just one look at 'Cyril's' minute mapping pen script, made a face of dismay and said pleadingly, 'Could you read it for me?' I did my best and it was quite difficult even for me, who was used to it. After I had finished, she was sweet enough to spend at least five minutes talking to us both, although I could see that her dressing room was full of people (including Sol Hurok) all waiting to talk to her. The girl was thrilled and I must say I was quite pleased too. Such was Fonteyn's regard for Mr B.

From time to time in those days, I would have short periods of feeling 'depressed' (according to my journal). I cannot imagine why, since I had what I thought of as about the best job in the world, I was in good health and, although short of money, the occasional fee for this or that would tide me over. However, the least suggestion of such a state concerned Mr B greatly. I think he thought I might go into a decline and he would lose me. One morning when I had appeared a bit mopish he said, 'I'm trying hard to think of something to cheer you up', and went off home to have lunch. He returned later with a handkerchief soaked in Spanish eau de cologne sent to him by Roberto Ximenez. 'There', he said, 'That should do the trick.' It did. Bless him.

A few days later I had lunch with the aforementioned medical student, Michael Stoughton, who was at that time little more than an acquaintance. However, anxious to please, he had brought me a large box of strawberries as well as giving me lunch. I took them back to the shop and showed them to Mr B, telling him as delicately as I could who had given them to me. Off he went to lunch and returned with a large carton of cream, not to be outdone I could tell. We spent the afternoon clearing a shelf which was overcrowded and unusable. I received a few mementos including a proof copy of his *The Ballet called Swan Lake*. There were some enchanting little objects there – a four leaf clover picked by Taglioni and given to the young Margaret Rolfe, an original Alfred Chalon lithograph, and a ribbon from one of Pavlova's bouquets.

There was to be a Critics' Circle Luncheon in January 1955 at which Svetlana Beriosova had been invited to make a small speech. She came to Mr B in a panic: 'Please help me,' she begged, 'I've no idea of what to say.' He comforted her by promising to write what he called 'a few words' for her to learn. He showed them to me and asked, as he often did, for my opinion. I made a couple of small suggestions which he accepted and told Svetlana that he and I had written it together, which wasn't quite true but pleased her. She promised to learn them 'straight away'.

The next night after *Firebird*, I went round to see her. I told her about the 'fracas' of which she had heard nothing, and then, after a few derogatory remarks about one of Mr B's adversaries, said that she would repeat her 'small speech' to me. 'I'm word perfect' she said. 'You listen' and then proceeded to declaim the words with more pauses and ums and ers than actual words. It was quite funny. 'Mr B wrote you a few words,' I said 'but not one of them was UM or ER. Now, you really must concentrate. You don't want to let him down.' She looked at me with large eyes, suddenly realising her responsibility. 'I promise I'll learn it by Friday IMPECCABLY.'

In the end, it appears that the tiny speech (Mr B's and my combined efforts) went 'splendidly'. Among such luminaries as Gerald Moore, Robert Morley and J B Priestley, that was quite something.

CHAPTER NINE

Just after the Critics' Circle Luncheon, Mr B, knowing that I was going to *Rinaldo and Armida* that evening, asked me if I would take notes for him to help with his writing it up for his Third Supplement (to the *Complete Book of Ballets*, later to be called *Ballets Past and Present*). I had a firm conviction that I would do so; I promised that I would and I took my notepad with me, but in the interval I met Lilyne Beriosova (at that time Svetlana's step-mother) who told me that she (Svetlana) had had only had one rehearsal since it was last done three weeks before. And then the whole thing was so lovely and so heart-rending that I completely forgot about making notes. Afterwards, in the interval, I went round and found Svetlana in a state of pure joy. As usual, her first question was 'Was it all right?' I always told her the truth, as she knew I would, otherwise she would never have asked me.

I told her of my predicament – my promise to Mr B and my completely blank notepad. 'Come on,' she said, 'I'll tell you what to put'. She did, and so the roles were reversed as it were. She also told me with great pride how well her 'speech' had gone the day before. 'Not one um' she said.

Mr B was later elected Vice-President of the Critics' Circle which pleased him considerably.

****

One day when I was alone, Mr B having gone to the Sophie Fedorovitch Memorial Exhibition, I had a very exciting visitor – a member of the theatrical company (which one, I wonder?) which had taken *Hamlet* to Moscow came into the shop. We were able to have a long and uninterrupted conversation without my being aware of disapproval oozing through the office door. He not only described the performance of *Romeo and Juliet*, which they had seen at the Bolshoi, but produced one of Ulanova's shoes which she had worn during the performance. Her name was written on the sole and as I held the shoe in my hand I felt as if I were talking to someone who had visited Mars! The weight of the shoe was exactly four ounces, including the ribbons which were not actually ribbons at all, but coarse pink tapes. The block was about the same size and weight as that of shoes worn in this country and the shape of the shoe almost the same except that the vamp was cut in a V-shape. Inside it was lined with coarse hessian and outside, round the pointe, could be seen the remains of darning done in white cotton. It bore a much greater similarity to English shoes than either American or French, although the quality was poor. What a *frisson* that gave me.

On Mr B's return, I told him all this in detail. 'I quite envy you', he said.

****

Once a year, upon Mr B's departure for the Edinburgh Festival, I was given a thin booklet made of a folded sheet of foolscap paper (larger than the later A4) and covered in closely written notes, headed: 'Directions For Isabelle'.

These were my work directions for the days of his absence. Every regular customer who might come in and want to know if his order was in, or we had been able to obtain something not easily obtained, was written there under a name-heading, and a description of what we had done or not yet been able to do was described beneath.

For example: Mr Alexander: You will remember that the copies of *Arts* for Mr Alexander are on the top of the till; they are 11d each. To them, please add this week's copy also I think on the till, or on the blue case in the back room which Mr Morris got for me. There are also some copies of *Arts* etc. to be returned to Mr Dessau – they are usually marked with a 'D' in top right hand corner, and some copies of *Match* and *Times Lit Supplement*.

There was 'stock to be ordered', directions to the Typewriter Co, *Clique*, his address in Edinburgh, various addresses of people who might need to be contacted... most people would have needed several sheets of foolscap to encompass this immense quantity of information set out in his one. Even although I was used to Mr B's writing, my eyes still swam as I ploughed through this lot... and then, at the bottom of page four, I saw: *Envoi* I hope that all these notes will not prove too much for you to deal with. Just do what you can – I know you will do your best and that is saying a great deal CWB.

And all was forgiven.

****

Some time in the middle of 1954 the firm 'C W Beaumont' had been approached by Royal Mail Lines for suitable pictures of dancers to appear on their cruise menus. The obvious choice of photographer was my good and dear friend Roy Round, whose company, Fact Photography, was in Soho, walking distance away from 75. Roy was more than happy to undertake the business of taking interesting ballet pictures and produced a number of colour transparencies (which was the way things were done then). Six of the best results were chosen by Royal Mail and they agreed to pay 20 guineas a time (a lot of money then).

I gather from my journal that it was I who finalised the deal after spending 'a long time with Mr Dice of Royal Mail'. The total fee received for the three of us – CWB for the introduction, Roy for the photography and myself for the business 'chat' amounted to £126. I record somewhere that I received £7 2s and also it appeared that the more Royal Mail took (including, it seems, some by Paul Wilson) the more commission I would receive. By such means did I eke out my slender salary. Roy's productions included one of Svetlana Beriosova in *Sleeping Beauty*, another of Violetta Elvin also in *Sleeping Beauty*, Violette Verdy in the 'Blue Bird' pas de deux, and one of Antonio, the great Spanish dancer, to whom, and to his Company, I was much attached and about whom Mr B wrote a book. During the 1954 season at the Stoll Theatre, the Front of House Manager complained that chocolate sales had dropped drastically because everyone was spending their money on the book!

While Mr B was noticeably wary of my friendship, or even acquaintance, of anyone of the male sex, looking – as he would call it – ASKance at anyone speaking more than twenty words to me, dear Roy was excused. This was, supposedly, because he was my colleague in a professional capacity (apart from the Royal Mail enterprise I used to do some clothes modelling for Roy) and therefore above suspicion. Had he but known the extent of our friendship, my employer would not have been quite so sanguine. At one time we saw a great deal of each other, even buying a joint wedding present for Peter Wright and Sonya Hana, and going to the wedding together.

But, once more, it was 'what the eye doesn't see'...

CHAPTER TEN

Two incidents concerned with 'rescue by taxi' stay in my mind. The first happened in November 1954 when the Japanese Ballet Company of Miho Hanayagui were performing at the Prince's Theatre. One evening, on his way home in the pouring rain, Mr B came across three of the dancers huddled together in a forlorn group in Cambridge Circus. With no protection whatever from the downpour, their wonderful robes were getting soaked. At last – having failed by conventional means to secure a taxi – the gallant Mr B stepped boldly in front of a cab, whose 'FOR HIRE' flag was covered by a glove (the accepted sign that the driver had finished for the day). He explained the position to the driver, who said that although he was going home he would take them all to the Prince's Theatre. I'm quite sure that he was very well paid for the favour. On arrival, their rescuer hustled them through the stage door where they were met by someone (their manager?) who appeared to be in charge and who, although he spoke no English, offered money to pay the fare. It was refused by Mr B (graciously, I am sure) so the man produced a paper and pencil and asked for his name (how? I wonder). After Mr B had obliged, the man suddenly whipped a tiny fan from a pocket and presented it with much bowing and Eastern courtesy and smiles from the three who had been rescued.

****

I have still a folder containing something approaching a hundred letters, notes, Christmas cards, birthday cards and cards which came with presents from Mr B. Our correspondence continued until just before he died, by which time the minute manuscript had become, mercifully, a little larger. The letters include one to 'Dear Mr Stoughton', written in February 1956 by which time the said Mr Stoughton was a frequent visitor to 75 Charing Cross Road and also a purchaser of expensive books. It would appear that after the first night of *La Péri* poor Mr B had felt 'rather ill'. Seeing my concern, the ubiquitous Mr Stoughton had rushed out of the Opera House, secured a taxi, and told the driver to wait. Then, between us, we got *The Sunday Times* ballet critic, (for that was why he was there) aboard and on his way home. An attack of bronchitis followed, keeping him to his bed for some time. I, apparently, was given a basket of oranges to take on my next visit to 68 Bedford Court Mansions. 'The fruit', the letter states, 'was most helpful and although I cannot say that I am well, I certainly feel better.'

It must have been a bad attack because the doctor was called. Once, when I was away with a severe cold (not surprising when the temperature at 75 often felt like sub-zero) he wrote to me: 'Do see the doctor. As Sir Osbert says "seeing the doctor shifts the responsibility".'

****

Some time before I arrived at 75, Mr B wrote a letter to Richard Buckle, editor of the monthly magazine *Ballet*.

The subject being formal, the letter was typewritten and concerned an article on the late Nicholas Legat, once a well-known teacher of ballet, and an advertisement of the latter's school, which operated in London at that time.

I quote it in full:

Dear Mr Buckle,

Although I am included in the Associated Editors of *Ballet* I would like to make it clear to your readers that this position is purely honorary and not executive. In the latter instance I should not permit any advertiser to be described as the 'World's Most Famous Teacher of Ballet' – however, that is by the way.

I notice that in the current issue for January there is an article by A. B. on a distinguished figure in the history of Russian Ballet – the late Nicholas Legat. In that article your contributor, commenting upon Legat's London School, which at one time was situated in Colet Gardens, states the school 'became a haunt of well known critics like Richardson, Haskell and Beaumont'. Permit me to observe that so far from *haunting* the Legat school I have never even set foot inside it.

Again, in the advertisement of the present Legat School, it is asserted that the Legat System has produced a number of well-known dancers including Pavlova, Nijinsky, Lifar, Massine, Dolin, Markova, Ashton and Turner.

It is a common practice for all dancers in the course of their career to study with a variety of teachers according to convenience and to where professional engagement takes them, because it is imperative for them to keep in training so long as they dance. For this reason it is extremely difficult to state with certainty that a particular dancer has obtained all her training with a specific teacher. If each teacher could claim as pupil every dancer who attended a class in his or her studio, such claims would soon reach the bounds of absurdity.

If, therefore, it is desired to establish which teacher has contributed most to the formation of a certain dancer, it is usual to accord the credit to the teacher who first prepared a pupil in his or her studio for actual appearance on the stage.

Pavlova and Nijinsky were both products of the Imperial Ballet School attached to the Maryinsky Theatre St Petersburg, where a whole staff of teachers combined to bring out the best in each pupil. It is a fact, however, that Pavlova sought to bind Cecchetti under contract to be her 'exclusive teacher'. Nijinsky also had a high opinion of Cecchetti, and studied under him.

Lifar received his initial training in Kiev from Bronislava Nijinska, but, when he was admitted to the Diaghilev Ballet, he pleaded that he might study privately with Cecchetti, which the Director arranged. And when Cecchetti died, did not Lifar, when dancing that evening in *Les Sylphides* wear a black scarf as a sign of mourning for his revered teacher?

Massine began his training at the Moscow Dramatic School. On joining the Diaghilev Ballet he was likewise placed in the care of Cecchetti.

Markova and Dolin were both trained by the Princess Astafieva.

When Ashton, then a schoolboy, wished to study ballet, he asked me to suggest a teacher. I recommended him to go to Massine with whom he studied for a while, until the latter had to leave London on a professional engagement; he advised Ashton to continue his studies with Marie Rambert, which he did with results that everyone knows, for it was at the Ballet Club that he acquired a reputation both as a dancer and choreographer.

Turner learned his first steps at the Haine School, then he came to London and studied for some years with Marie Rambert who gave him his first important roles.

By what right then does your advertiser presume to claim the above mentioned dancers as products of the Legat System?

One more comment. In a recent circular advertising a performance by pupils of the Legat School, M. Legat is described as having been an 'Officer of the French Academy'. Such a position does not exist. This is clearly a mis-translation of the name of a French decoration, the group called 'Palmes Académiqes', which comprises two degrees: 'Officier d'académie', and its superior, 'Officier de l'instruction publique'. These are coveted honours, but they are not quite the same as being a Member of the French Academy, one of the 48 Immortals!

Yours sincerely,

Cyril Beaumont

It was published in full under the Editor's heading 'Haunting disclaimed'.

This is another example (although earlier than '*The Firebird* Fracas') of the amazing quality and quantity of the Beaumont brain. There was never any point in someone's trying to be clever and outwit him or, as in this case, to try to enhance the situation beyond its reality, because he always knew the facts far better than they did.

CHAPTER ELEVEN

LETTERS FROM EDINBURGH

North British Hotel
Edinburgh
26 August 1954

Dear Isabelle,

Thank you for your letter and for your loving kindness in looking after my wife as much as circumstances permit. I was most grateful to you, also for letting me know how she is. Thank you also for your closing message.

I am sorry that I had not had a moment to write before. I really have not had much time to myself, which may sound strange.

My wife was not at all well on Monday morning and I was in two minds about going, but as it was awkward to change all the arrangements, I just put my trust in you, as I always do, and went.

I arrived about five thirty, went to the hotel, arranged my things, had a wash and set out for the theatre. In the first interval I bowed to several smiling faces, not knowing who they were, and also met several people I did know, such as Serge Lifar who had come the day before to the Diaghilev Exhibition and stayed for the opening night of the ballet. It was rather swell with the Lord Provost wearing a jewelled badge on a ribbon about his neck, and other dignitaries with their badges of office.

I had a nice seat and with me sat Cyril King. I forgot to mention that on coming up into the ground floor from the station, I met Ninette. Then just as I was going to the theatre I met Michael Wood in the lounge, who took me to Caryl Brahms. I went in their taxi to the theatre. It was pouring with rain.

During another interval Buckle came to see me – and now I shall make you envious – *and* he has asked me if I will come to the party afterwards, which was being given at the College of Art where the Diaghilev Exhibition is housed, and after supper he would show me over the exhibits.

I was a little tired but I agreed, wishing to see the Exhibits. We went in buses, a very precious load in ours, Ninette, Somes, Grigoriev, Tchernicheva, Wood and so on. I must say the supper was very good. It was held in the so-called Hall of Giants, where you sit to hear the music (broadcast from radiograms) of the Diaghilev Ballets. Down one side was a long table covered with white cloths and a splendid array of slices of cold beef, ham, tongue, turkey, potato salad, Russian salad, green salad, blancmange, cakes and so on. Champagne was also to be had for the asking. I sat at a table with Rowena Jackson and Chatfield and we talked ballet.

Buckle was very busy greeting guests and it was about twelve forty-five before one got towards the exhibition. Just as one had passed through it, Princess Anne and Prince Charles of Denmark arrived and I was presented to them. I then tried to get a taxi to go home to the hotel but taxis were not to be found at that time of night – about one thirty. So rather than hanging about, four of us resolved to walk it. I went with Plucis. It was raining, dark as pitch, and you might have been in the Middle Ages for all the light in the streets. All one could see was the great rocky mass on which Edinburgh Castle stands. I began to feel like Sylvia in Orion's cave. At last we got to High St and I began to have hopes of getting home. But you had better not tell my wife of this adventure. She would be very shocked to think that I had been strolling about Edinburgh at the dead of night. The things one gets up to when one is on one's own!

You asked me about *Firebird*. I do not care much for it as a choreographic work. It seems very dated. There are many soli for the ballerina and few *ensembles* and not much else. Stravinsky's music, however, is superb. I did not care much for Fonteyn in the title role. She dances very well but has an exotic make-up with sideburns à l'Espagnole and her rendering so far as interpretation is concerned seemed forced. I did not find scenes which used to be so moving at all touching. I am afraid I shall not be popular for my views on the production which is very colourful as regards scenery, though not poetic. You, not having seen the original Golovine setting, may think differently. But I speak as I find.

Nerina and Turner do the Can Can in *Boutique* passably but not like Lopokova and Massine – alas. Elvin is good in *Tricorne*, and Grant very fair as the Miller, but there are some steps of Zapateado which induce nerves and a sense of frustration. It all looks so easy when Antonio does scores, if not hundreds! It is another thing to do it oneself.

The Diaghilev Exhibition is really something and most touching to those familiar with the period. Buckle has really done marvels not only in the materials he has collected but in the way they are presented. Twenty galleries, each lined with different wallpaper on the walls and pictures, and with them desks painted to match, showing photos of the dancers in the actual costumes so you can compare the designs with the costume as worn.

What with writing about the ballet and the Exhibition which is too much to take in at one visit, struggling to rewrite the article to fit the required number of words and having a wire from the *Sunday Times* to do something else, which if all goes well you may see next Sunday, this is the first rest I have had. I had hoped to begin my holiday tomorrow.

Last night I went to see the Old Vic production of *Macbeth* which is very good indeed, and now I am off to see Harro Siegel's Puppets. I shall have much to tell you. Thank you again for looking after the shop and for keeping things going.

Gratefully and sincerely yours

Cyril Beaumont

****

North British Hotel
Edinburgh
29 August 1955
Dear Isabelle,

Thank you so much for your letter and for all your news. I am very glad that you did so well on Wednesday because, as you know, I have still some bills to pay! As you warned me, I must not expect this *every* day but I shall of

Isabelle Stoughton

Telephone:
Waverley 2414
Private Box No. 79

NORTH BRITISH HOTEL

EDINBURGH 2

Sunday

Dear Isabelle. Thank you so much for your letter and for all your news. I am very glad that you did so well on Wednesday, because as you know I have told some bills to pay. As you warn me, I must not expect this every day, but I shall of course hope that the pace will be maintained. You should have a visit from that group [of] students who are interested in Lawson's European Folk Dance, and I hope some good will result if their visit materializes. I feel a little guilty being here and leaving every thing to your capable hands. But I have been pretty busy here.

No sooner did I arrive that I had tea and a tidy up and then off to the theatre to see "La Sylphide" and the new ballet "Capriccios Lucinda". The first I love and Schanne & Ravelens are just as good as ever. Schanne is delightful and so lyrical and expression. The other work is not very good, although it includes two of those attractive divertissements.

On my arrival I found a long telegram from the S.T. wanting me to send two articles to reach them Friday morning. So I had to set to work Thursday morning, then went to the office here and typed out about twice as much, back to lunch, and then worked on cutting down, back to office to retype and finally got the notice off at the G.P.O. then at 5 p.m.

After the Wednesday performance I met Volkova coming out, and she took me back stage to meet many [of] the men dancers, Schanne and Ravelens had gone home. I learned there was to be a rehearsal of "Romeo & Juliet" on Friday morning and was told they would be happy for me to attend. So I went to the theatre course *hope* that the pace will be maintained. You should have a visit from that group of students who were interested in Lawson's *European Folk Dance* and I hope some good will result if their visit materialises.

I feel a little guilty being here and leaving everything to your capable hands, but I have been pretty busy here.

No sooner did I arrive than I had I tea and a tidy up and then off to the theatre to see *La Sylphide* and the new ballet *Capricious Lucinda*. The first I love and Schanne and Kronstam are just as good as ever. Schanne is delightful and so lyrical and expressive. The other work is not very good, although it includes two or three attractive divertissements.

On my arrival I found a long telegram from the ST wanting me to send 400 words to reach them Friday morning. So I had to set to work Thursday morning, then went to the office here and typed out about twice as much, back to lunch, and then worked on cutting down, back to office to retype and finally got the notice off at the G.P.O here at 5pm.

After the Wednesday performance I met Volkova coming out and she took me back stage to meet many of the men dancers, Schanne and Kronstam had gone home. I learned there was to be a rehearsal of *Romeo and Juliet* on Friday morning and was told they would be happy for me to attend. So I went to the theatre at 10.15am. The rehearsal went on to nearly 2pm. The stage has insufficient depth and the lighting was sketchy. I think the chief electrician, after working at an afternoon lighting rehearsal, had to go home feeling knocked out. The setting is based on round platforms, combined with steps and curtains, and the changes are tricky. Some of the costumes are very nice.

The ballet is on a modest scale but the actions of the lovers from their first meeting to their deaths are most clearly explained and with an unusual economy of means. All the other characters are so presented that you grasp their character at once.

This is not a big scale work like a Covent Garden production, but viewed with a sense of proportion and making allowances for lack of lighting equipment and the (illegible), it is certainly the best of Ashton's full length ballets. The ballroom ensemble in which the dancers wear great flowing dresses which billow and spread – form a fine contrast to the men in doublet and hose who have falling scalloped sleeves which flutter in their movements.

The Romeo is a very romantic looking young man with a yearning look in his eyes. He is called Henning Kronstam. The Juliet is Mona Vangsaae who gives a fine performance. How Svetlana would adore this role! You see Juliet first as a young girl playing rather childishly with her nurse, until Lady Capulet enters, followed by a page with a mirror. Juliet is bidden to look within and attention drawn to her budding breasts, intimating that she must think of marriage. Juliet evinces a maidenly alarm at the prospect but seems resigned until she meets Romeo at the Ball. The scene which Vangsaae shows her wavering between shyness and first love and the balcony scene when she longs for a sight of Romeo only to be afraid when he does come, followed by a love scene which becomes more and more intense is really most moving. This Pas de Deux and another in the bedroom scene, when she tries to delay Romeo's leaving her, are most effective.

In the balcony scene the two lovers fondle each other with open mouths pressed against every part of the face and neck that can be reached. I see that Mr B[uckle] was rather shaken by this; contrary wise, I found this approach rather subtle. It is like two puppies loving to kiss each other, but without expertise or desire to arouse erotic feelings, it is such joy to put their faces in actual contact.

Juliet wears a simple white dress, relieved with a fall of pale blue ribbon. Her dances are based on lifts and turns, pas de bourré and the arabesque line with lyrical movements of the arms.

But given the time, I could write yards about Romeo and Juliet. The fight scenes, though brief, are quite exciting because the blades whistle through the air and the men, being Danes, use the swords with a very business like air. Larsen is a very venomous, sneering, Tybalt. The dying in his case and that of Mercutio is over long but rather a difficult scene to change. Prokofiev visualised the duels thus, and it would be difficult to cut the music. There is, however, an ensemble dance for Verona citizens which is rather weak.

Saturday morning I had a chat with Mr Jacobsen who is staying here, actually about two rooms from me. Then I had to telephone my account of Romeo to the ST with spelling out Danish names. Again I had written too much and my article has been cut. But I hope it did not read too badly.

Today the Danish Ballet was invited to spend the day touring the Highlands and late Saturday night I had a telephoned invitation to join them. Having no business I could do on Sunday I agreed. We went in three coaches, starting at 10am and got back at 8pm. It was a lovely journey through wonderful *Sylphide* country, and we stopped at Perth for lunch. It was a lovely hotel with a huge room and many tables to accommodate the 90 odd personnel, dancers and technical staff. The tables were each decorated with a vase of red and white flowers. The representation of the Danish firm that organised the day made speeches, to which the Director of the Royal Theatre responded and the proceedings concluded with the Ballet Co's special 'cheer'.

I hardly dare to mention the menu because you will be really envious of my good fortune – Scotch Broth, Tay Salmon and salad, Roast Beef, peas and potatoes, Fruit and Ice Pudding, coffee.

Now and again during the journey we stopped to see the scenery and for what one Dane told me 'covenances' a word I could not understand, but afterwards found he meant conveniences! We stopped at Loch Earn, a lovely spot, a great stretch of water with a surface like glass and hills rising high upwards, the distant ones veiled in mist.

Later we stopped at another place where we had a wonderful tea – scones, biscuits and pastries.

Volkova sat by me part of the way and we had a very interesting chat about all sorts of ballet problems at home and abroad.

Thank you for taking the flowers to my wife and for looking after her and keeping her as cheerful as possible under the circumstances. It would be nice if you were here because I could now show you something of the city where I feel quite at home. I am even a little sorry that I cannot sport a tartan.

Although, as you know, I sent some of the principals telegrams of good wishes, what seems to have pleased most was the telegram to the children. I am very fond of them, although they are not the ones I met during the London season. They came with us on the tour today and I have given them a few shillings each to buy what sweets they like. They each came forward and thanked me with a handshake and a little bow.

They are very well behaved except for one instance, which you must not repeat. It seems that one of the boys, wandering about the auditorium, took hold of one of the fire extinguishers and aiming it at another boy pressed the button in fun and scattered the seats with a fire extinguishing powder which took hours to clean up.

I hope that your mother is feeling better as a result of her diet and that your friend is making progress towards recovery.

Yours very sincerely

Cyril Beaumont

CHAPTER TWELVE

The Diaghilev Exhibition, transferred from Edinburgh to Forbes House in London in November 1954, was a splendid collection of items and artefacts relating to Diaghilev and superbly displayed. Richard Buckle had excellent artistic taste in matters of decoration and how to show his collection (much of it borrowed from 75 Charing Cross Road) to its best advantage. There was continuous playing of music from the Diaghilev ballets which added to the pleasure. I took with me the nine-year-old Alexandra Kirsta on my first visit.

A few days later I went again. Mr B was giving a talk on Diaghilev, about whom he knew a great deal. Most of what he said I knew already because he used to tell me quite often about those magical days. But, he said tentatively, that he hoped that I would go as he would feel 'comfortable' if I were there. Even though I had heard it all – or most of it – before, I was enchanted to hear him speak to a great room full of people, all listening with eagerness and interest.

After the Exhibition had closed and the borrowed items returned, Mr B offered me the choice of several costume designs for Sadko by Boris Anisfeld. I chose one and I still have it. Others were sold to customers so that by the time Anisfeld's family arrived, anxious to buy the prints at any price, there were only two left.

****

Ashton's *Cinderella*, which was such a delight to watch, especially when Fonteyn danced, had – as a comical element – Cinderella's two step-sisters played by Ashton and Kenneth MacMillan. At first this male duo was amusing and very cleverly nuanced by the two men. Ashton's original portrayal of the rather pathetic middle aged spinster, timid and frustrated, completely dominated by the elder sister, was admirable. Gradually, however, he added little touches above and beyond the choreography and finally overstepped the limit to which may be gone in character-ballet and made of the part a clown pantomime-dame, more suited to twentieth century Palladium than eighteenth century France. Finally the performance became so camp that I could not even watch. Mr B had commented on all this, somewhat mildly it is true, in his article. We talked about it on the Monday and he said 'It only wants his knickers to fall off when he is presented to the prince and that is about all there is left to happen.' I laughed and said 'Why don't you suggest it to him?' 'Good God NO' he replied, 'He'd do it!'

****

I went to the first night of Martha Graham in March 1954 and found it not my kind of thing at all. Talking to Mr B next, he dismissed it as 'A lot of nonsense'.

One day in the summer of 1955, Mr B and I were talking about Markova and how incredibly light she was. I started to tell him about the time when she appeared as the celebrity in 'What's My Line?' (a TV panel game of the time), and the panel guessed immediately that it was a dancer because she trod so lightly when she came in that they could not hear her and then Isobel Barnett said 'I know – it's Madam Markova'. At that moment our telephone rang; I answered and a voice said 'It's Madam Markova'. I was almost too astonished to speak! When she came in a couple of days later to take Mr B out to lunch, I told her the story and she was quite startled, then laughed and said 'The Wilis must be at work!'

****

Mr B and his young Icelandic friend had some sort of difference (perhaps misunderstanding would be a better word) over what, I never knew. He appeared distressed and dejected and told me sadly of how he felt. He really did love that girl – how he would have loved a musical daughter. I said what comforting words I could summon. 'I tell you everything', he said, adding 'Well, almost everything'. I think it was a relief for him to have someone to tell who could be trusted not to repeat things, who was sympathetic and never shocked. Whether the difference, or 'misunderstanding' was ever resolved, I do not now remember.

****

When the second supplement to the *Complete Book of Ballets* came out in 1954, Mr B gave me one of the few advance jackets, bearing the title *Ballets of Today*. I was quite pleased because I had been partly responsible for it. When Putnam's first produced the jacket it was a lurid affair of red, yellow and green checks with a drawing (none too flattering) of Roland Petit in *Le Loup*. When Mr B asked me if I liked it, my answer was an emphatic 'NO'. He himself was not at all impressed by it and thought we should alter it before Putnam's got used to it. So he suggested I look through some *Ballet Annuals* and find something more suitable. I found a picture from *Homage to the Queen* which gave him the idea of another picture from *Homage* with Fonteyn and Somes, which I got from somewhere and finally the jacket appeared, pale blue with a picture of them both, large and plain. We felt rather pleased with ourselves.

****

A book by A H Franks (Deputy Editor of *Dancing Times*) called *Ballet, a Decade of Endeavour*, consisted of essays by various people. In one of them a man called Wray referred to Mr B as 'The greatest living ballet critic' which pleased him very much. He was not however, so pleased that the same man stated that he 'came a cropper over his criticism of *Firebird*'. Obviously Mr Wray had not followed the argument – or the *Sunday Times* correspondence – through to the end or he would have known that it was certainly not CWB who came a cropper!

****

It was in the spring of 1956 (25 April to be precise) that the Royal Opera House was visited by Nikolai Bulganin and Nikita Khrushchev, Prime Minister and President respectively of the Soviet Union. According to my journal 'A great deal of to-do was made, Bow Street being so thickly lined with police that there would not have been room for an assassin to get between them. No cars were allowed except those people entering the Opera House, and inside there was a throng of press men. Lights were so strong that they made the place like a furnace and every seat opposite the Royal Box was occupied by Russian Security Police, masquerading as journalists. The occupants of the Royal Box – 'B and K' as they were irreverently known – were dressed in very casual clothes while everyone else was in evening dress. Michael and I were the only people allowed in seats opposite them because we had a season ticket, but we, I believe, had been cleared by Scotland Yard. I noticed that when I opened my handbag to extract a handkerchief, the 'journalists' on either side of us went into Alert Mode, thinking perhaps that I might draw a gun. Amused by this, I made a point of opening the bag several times just to see their reaction. It was always the same.

Rowena Jackson later filled me in with all the backstage news regarding the 'B and K Night'. Everyone assembled backstage to meet them after the performance. But, instead of getting on and introducing each one, Madam insisted on waiting for Margot, who was ten minutes late. At last, Violetta arrived and Madam seized her because, of course, being Russian, she spoke Russian, and presented her to Bulganin. He misunderstood her identity and thought she was Fonteyn and the conversation begun to get rather involved. Suddenly Violetta turned round and in her heavily-accented Russian English said, 'My God, he think I *am* Margot! What I do now?'

The gifts to the Company were, I believe, lavish: and included cigarettes, chocolates and brandy.

All this I told to Mr B who relished all the bits of backstage news and gossip with which I frequently regaled him. 'Just think of all the friends you make here', he said, as if it were a benediction. And I did think of them, frequently.

CHAPTER THIRTEEN

During the autumn of 1955, the 'Pavlova Commemoration Committee' was formed. It consisted of a number of dancers who had been with her company, Michael Wood, Arnold Haskell and several others and Mr B as Chairman. Its aim was to produce a Commemoration Performance of the 25th anniversary of Pavlova's death. It was to take place at midnight on 23 January at the Stoll Theatre and would be performed by artists from many parts of the world. It was hoped that some members of Royalty would attend. Quite quickly, Fonteyn, Marjorie Tallchief, Skibine and Chauviré all promised to appear and invitations had been sent out to many more.

There was a Miss Rita Glynde who had danced with Pavlova, and who started off quite forcefully as 'She who must be obeyed.' She had tremendous energy which soon began to get on Mr B's nerves, I could tell. He insisted on calling her 'Miss Glynde – I'm not having any of this Rita and Cyril stuff' he said quite early on. The whole business began to take up more and more of Mr B's time, and mine as well. I have to say for Rita Glynde that if it had not been for her fantastic mental and physical energy I doubt if the idea would ever had reached fruition. But things began to get tiresome: Haskell, having agreed to be on the Committee, did not turn up to one single meeting. Markova and Chauviré both announced their intention of dancing *La*

Cygne and both had to be dissuaded. Markova then refused to say what she would be doing instead.

The BBC, it was rumoured, were making a television
programme about Pavlova, but no one from that organi-
sation had asked any member of the Committee for any
details about her and refused to discuss the script when
asked, merely stating that their own script-writers would
be dealing with it. One wondered what they could possibly know and it was suspected that the whole thing would
be in bad taste.

Mr B urged me several times to be sure to record every
detail in my journal. The arrangement of the programme
was in his hands. He had asked Elsa Marianne von Rosen
and Björn Holmgren from Sweden to do the pas de deux,
Flower Festival in Genzano. It was really Danish (choreographed by August Bournonville) but happened to be
something they knew and performed well and of which
Mary Skeaping (their Maitresse de Ballet, who was in
London at the time) approved. No one from Denmark
could come, owing to some special performance of their
own. Toni Lander from Festival Ballet was invited to rep-
resent the Danes, being herself Danish, and to bring John
Gilpin as her partner. This meant their returning from
Monte Carlo, where Festival Ballet then had a season, for
three days. They chose, with Mr B's full approval, a pas de
deux which Harald Lander had set and later put into
Napoli which they both did very well. By the merest
chance it was suddenly discovered that these two pas de
deux were one and the same thing! Confusion reigned for
several days, Elsa Marianne and Holmgren had gone, at
their own expense, to Copenhagen to have special coach-

ing from the ballet master there, and were, not unnaturally, very upset when they heard the news.

Similarly, Toni Lander was loath to give it up, since her husband had arranged it and she was Danish anyway. Dolin, Festival Ballet's Director, was very keen for them to do it. Mary Skeaping, on the other hand, refused to sanction her dancers doing anything in which she had not coached them. Cables, express letters and telephone calls flew about frantically, and at last it was settled that Toni Lander and Gilpin should have the honour and the Swedes would have to do something else.

Markova refused to decide until the last possible moment what she would do if denied *La Cygne*, or if she had decided, refused to say. In the end she announced, somewhat reluctantly, that she would do *Bolero 1830* with the proviso that no one else must do anything Spanish. With difficulty, Dolin was persuaded that it would be best for everybody if he only spoke, since it seemed possible that he might dance his own (quite terrible) *Bolero*. Ram Gopal came to see Mr B saying that he was really representing Asia, and not just India and did his best to make a fuss about where he should appear in the programme. He was, as things stood, doing two solos to everyone else's one, and finally Mr B who was not feeling at all well at the time and retired to his bed with flu the next day, said that if he heard any more about it he would take him – Gopal – out of the programme altogether.

It began to seem as if only a few people were thinking of the great artist to whom they were paying homage, and the rest were only thinking of themselves, and the degree of importance they thought should have been attached to them.

On the Friday afternoon before the performance, Freddy Ashton waltzed into the shop and said, in a very mincing voice, 'I've just come to say that I'll only come to the Pavlova Matinée if I can dance *The Swan*' and we had a little giggle because it was obvious whom he was sending up.

At that point I was left in charge of the ordering of the ribbons for the bouquets and the printing thereon. It does not sound much but was in fact quite detailed and took several telephone hours. I was already having to take quite a lot of responsibility from Mr B's shoulders, confined as he was to his bed. But this was nothing compared with what was to come.

I was beginning to feel the strain. There was not only the shop to cope with and the correspondence and orders and all the usual things, but everything relating to the programme on Monday night. Mr B who, with Michael Wood, was in charge of the designing of the printed programme, had said to me quite unequivocally from his bed the previous day that the giving of instructions to the printer and the final word in all things relating to the programme must be left to him, since he had the technical knowledge of such things, and Michael Wood the experience of producing Gala programmes. Miss Glynde, praiseworthy in some respects, had never liked his design; she and the Committee wanted something far more elaborate – a white and gold cover, silk cords etcetera, which would have cost a fortune. On Tuesday morning she rang me and said that Gorlinsky (the impresario who had seen two or three page-proofs when Michael Wood sent the printer to see him) had telephoned her 'screaming' that it was all terrible and MUST be altered or he would not have his name put to it. I tried not to feel unjustly towards Rita Glynde, but it did seem to me that her attitude was to seize the opportunity to step in during Mr B's absence and to alter things to suit her own wishes. She said 'The programme is so terrible that now Mr Beaumont is ill I think it must be taken out of his hands. He'll be angry at first, poor old man, but he'll soon get over it. I'll go and see him and smooth him down. I've spoken to Mr Franks and he is going to get larger blocks made and I want you to find out as many biographical details as you can and I'll come in and collect them later'... And there was a lot more unrecorded. I was aghast because I knew for one thing that Mr B would be furious. So, she rang again to see if I had collected biographies of the artists appearing and added that I had 'better not mention this to Mr Beaumont in case it upsets him'. Then I discovered that she had rung the printer and given fresh instructions. I told her quite firmly that I could not help her; my first loyalty was to Mr Beaumont and that if she was going to go behind his back as soon as he was ill, she had better not tell me about it, because if I knew I could never look him in the face again. She was amazed and not too pleased.

I was sitting at the desk, trying to make sense of the whole situation, when suddenly a large picture fell off the wall behind me, the glass shattering as it reached the floor. A framed poster of the Camargo Society had met its doom. I remembered my grandmother saying that when a picture fell down and smashed, it predicted someone's death. At that moment, I felt that it might well be mine.

Then, like a bolt from Heaven, Michael Wood rang and I told him the whole sad story. He said that I must go and tell Mr B everything. He was very kind and helpful and said that he would telephone Gorlinsky himself, which was a great relief. So off I went to Bedford Court Mansions to tell Mr B what had happened. He was, as I had expected, very upset and hurt and angry that Miss G could act in so underhand a manner but I knew that Michael Wood had been right to say that I must tell him. The next morning I rang the printer and gave him orders about his instructions, (the day before the poor man had received *five* different sets of instructions from five different people!) and I told him that, as from that minute when I was speaking, he was to disregard any orders that did not come from Mr Wood or Mr Beaumont via me, or we should not have a programme at all. And finally it looked as if we were beginning to get somewhere, although I discovered that Miss Glynde had made one more attempt to get what she described as 'The Committee's wishes' and had been in further consultation with Gorlinsky. So I rang the man myself and found him rather as I had expected him to be – forceful, argumentative and Jewish. It was like playing a game with him because every time he blustered at me I countered him by saying 'I will of course, pass on all your comments to Mr Beaumont'. It must have been, for him, like being hit with a feather pillow and after a while he gave up all attempts at bullying and listened to me with at least a degree of politeness.

It was all very unpleasant and I had felt for a time as if the responsibility for the whole affair rested on my shoulders. Mr B became what he termed 'Nasty' ('I can get very nasty when I like'). He wrote a very strong letter to Rita Glynde ('Dear Miss Glynde') accusing her of wanting to have 'A finger in every pie'. This was a phrase which she found particularly humiliating and came to me in an attempt to cry on my shoulder and tell me how hurt she had been by it. I was not having any of that; I could get nasty too. Mr B announced his attention to resign from the Committee at once and to 'let them get on with it'.

More complications arose when Markova saw the programme and said that she would NOT have Chauviré dancing a solo immediately before her, and further more she would not have Nerina and Rassine dancing the pas de deux from *Don Quixote* when she had been promised faithfully that no one else would do anything Spanish. This was true and Nerina had been down originally to dance the Act III pas de deux from *Coppélia* with David Blair. It was changed at her request, probably because she felt that the *Quixote* showed her off to better advantage.

Markova's sister, Doris Barry, who was also her manager, came into the shop in a somewhat belligerent mood, and began a tirade in her sister's defence. She had some very harsh things to say about the way she (Markova) had been treated in London but was gracious enough to pause and tell me that of course it was not my fault. I offered to go and talk to Nadia (who was a close friend) and see if I could persuade her to revert to *Coppélia*, but I also pointed out the two solos were at opposite ends of the programme and totally different in style. She finally gave way on the matter of *Quixote* but remained adamant about Chauviré. However, my feeling was that when Chauviré saw the programme fireworks would ensue since, for one thing, she almost certainly regarded herself as an equal star to Markova and it was well known that the two loathed each other. I said to Miss Barry that I thought it a pity to see people fighting for supremacy among themselves when the real star of the evening died 25 years ago.

In contrast, Margot Fonteyn when asked what she would like to dance in the *divertissements* said 'As I'm already doing *Homage* at the end, I don't think I'd better do anything else. It might look as though we were trying to impress the importance of the Wells.' This attitude, so typical of her, was part of her greatness.

CHAPTER FOURTEEN

Midnight, Monday 23 January 1956. What a night! In the end, in spite of all the trials and squabbles and seemingly endless difficulties (including only one orchestra rehearsal) the performance was utterly brilliant and a triumph for everyone concerned. At the last minute I was asked to organise the 24 programme girls and we sold 2000 programmes and ran out of supplies. The House was packed, every seat taken and many people standing. The bouquets had arrived safely with their commemoration ribbons intact, and the specially-bound Pavlova books for the men arrived in time (at one point it had seemed that they would not) and everybody danced magnificently.

It was, however, a pity that Leighton Lucas had not rehearsed Tchaikowsky's *Romeo and Juliet* music for the pas de deux sufficiently with Mariane Orlando and Kenneth Petersen. So slowly did he take it that the poor dancers had to repeat the coda not once but twice. They were both very upset, unsurprisingly, and although the audience for the most part did not realise that anything was amiss and applauded solidly for five minutes, the two refused to return to the stage and take even one curtain. A pity to disappoint the audience, but that, I think, was the only slip-up of the evening.

Nerina and Rassine danced the *Don Quixote* pas de deux and although I, and at least half the people to whom I spoke afterwards, thought that she danced splendidly and that even *he* was bearable, the other half (Mr B included) thought that it was not good or even downright bad. I had to beg him to alter his *Sunday Times* article to make it read more pleasantly about her. It seemed very hard that while he had written so well, even glowingly of everyone else in the programme, he merely said of those two that they had 'danced Petipa's *Don Quixote* pas de deux'. After a lot of persuasion, because I thought she would be dreadfully upset if he just wrote that, he finally and reluctantly agreed to add 'to enthusiastic applause', which was true and did not entail his giving praise which he felt was un-justified (which he never would have done) and at least mitigated somewhat the bareness of the statement.

Ram Gopal's two dances left me quite cold but they made a contrast to the classical items in the programme. Elsa-Marianne von Rosen's little solo *La Lithuanienne*, was quite enchanting, and her purple and gold costume very attractive. Chauviré danced the variation from the *Grand Pas Classique* brilliantly, although she made a bad ending, but so slight that most people would not have noticed. Markova did *Bolero 1830* to complete perfection and her choice of it was clever because had she chosen a classical solo requiring a strong technique, she would have been placed immediately in comparison, probably to her disadvantage, with Chauviré, Fonteyn, Grey, Elvin, Beriosova and Nerina, all of whom had a stronger classical technique. I loved the *Night Shadow* pas de deux (danced by Marjorie Tallchief and George Skibine) and the Gilpin and Lander rendering of the *Flower Festival* pas de deux and Björn Holmgren's *Figaro* solo. *Les Sylphides*, with which the programme opened, looked strangely beautiful against the black velvet drapes and framed by the white Moorish arch which could not be removed as it was a permanent fixture for *Kismet* running at the Stoll at that time. I loved Svetlana's *Prelude* which she told me was a faithful following of Tchernicheva's instructions. At the end came 'Water' and 'Air' from *Homage to the Queen* and Margot very rightly and properly crowned the whole glittering performance.

Afterwards I collected Svetlana from the stage door; she looked desperately tired and a little sad, so I tucked her up in a rug in the back of the car and didn't say a great deal. She told me that she was exhausted; she said she had 'Danced with every ballerina'. When Chauviré felt the rake, she felt the rake too. When Petersen dropped Orlando, she fell too. She said it was very moving backstage and I could see that she had been crying 'Close your eyes,' I said, 'and don't talk'. After a couple of minutes of doing as I had said, she opened her eyes for long enough to say, 'I wonder how much Markova's flowers cost her?' and then dozed off again.

There had been moments in the time leading up to the performance where I had been stretched to the limit and had felt – perhaps rather dramatically – as if everything depended on me but in the end, it had all been worth it, everything had gone smoothly and all the dancers – while they may not actually have embraced each other – at least smiled at one another. The whole evening had been a triumph and people coming to the shop talked of nothing else for weeks.

The performance raised a profit of £1,350, £500 of which was paid into the Sadler's Wells Ballet Benevolent Fund; £500 for the endowment of a bed in the Great

Ormond Street Children Convalescent Home; £250 to the Westminster Central Reference Library for the inauguration of a special Pavlova Library; and £100 for the purchase and direction of a memorial plaque at the Royal Opera House.

****

Throughout the entire saga of the Pavlova Commemoration Committee, the performance and all the unpleasantness in between, Mr B had urged me to write meticulous details in my journal of all that was happening. He had not the time to do so himself but knew it was important to have everything recorded as he had intended to include it in his memoirs, when he had time to write them. (I asked him once who he would like to write his biography. He replied 'Sachie Sitwell, but you'd have to help him'. He knew my weakness for detail.) A letter he wrote to me in November 1975, thanking me for a birthday card, ends thus: '...It would be very nice to see you... Your journal sounds very interesting. I should like to refresh my memory of the scandalous episode of the Pavlova Commemoration Performance which at present escapes me.

Affectionately, Cyril Beaumont'

Almost twenty years after the event which had occupied him so painfully and so entirely, he could remember nothing about it.

CHAPTER 15

On 11 July 1956, I finally agreed to marry Michael Stoughton. Next day, slightly hesitantly, I told Mr B the news knowing that almost certainly he would not feel overjoyed at the prospect of my leaving. After all, I was (I had been told), his 'prop and mainstay' and at his somewhat advanced age (64) he might not find it easy to settle down with anyone else into the comfortable and amiable state in which we had existed for three years. Even so, the stricken look on his face when I told him said more than any words. He gave me his congratulations and then said: 'I suppose this means that you'll be leaving?' and at that moment I thought of calling the whole thing off because I couldn't bear to hurt him. He, however, immediately took pen and paper and composed a letter of great civility and sincerity to the cause of all the trouble. He wrote:

Dear Mr Stoughton,

Isabelle told me today that she had just become engaged to you. I cannot withhold my admiration at the perseverance with which you have pursued your courtship, with results that have fully justified your faith in yourself and your deep love which I feel you have for her.

Permit me to offer you my sincere congratulations, for although your gain will eventually mean my loss – for I shall lose an assistant who has been of the greatest help to me – her happiness must be the first consideration. I hope that you will both enjoy every happiness.

Believe me.

Sincerely yours,

Cyril Beaumont

If only I could have been married and still worked for Mr B. In the 1950s, it was not the usual thing for married women to work unless they were in a profession or had financial need. Neither case applied to me but, nevertheless, had we been able to find a house in London that we could have afforded, I could have continued to travel to 75 Charing Cross Road daily or even half-daily. But property in London then was, as it is now, dearer than further afield and a very attractive cottage in Battersea cost £6,000, well beyond our means.

At last a large farmhouse in Thames Ditton was found at an affordable price (£3,500) and 'commuting', as it came to be called, was not possible. This seemed to be an end to both our hopes.

I was touched that he minded so much and I determined to keep him in my life for as long as I could. There were visits, letters, Christmas cards, birthday cards and presents for years afterwards, and these continued almost until his death.

He has had a lasting influence on my life and was both my teacher and my inspiration.

EPILOGUE

Every time I wrote a letter to a magazine or newspaper, every contribution to *Dancing Times'* 'Sitter Out' and any article I wrote for that magazine or for *Dance and Dancers*, I would ask Mr B to read and give his verdict on its suitability. Sometimes he would make a suggestion for some slight alteration or amendment, but usually pronounce it 'Very well constructed. I hope that will please you'.

From time to time, for example in the inscription on the fly-leaf of a book being given to me as a present, or a birthday or Christmas gift of another kind, or of the purchase of a book at trade price, Mr B would say 'I hope this will please you', and whatever it was it always did. He suggested that I should write a book about my days at 75. 'It would be very interESTing' he would say.

And now, after somewhat more that half a century, I have.

****

Somewhere in that section of Heaven which is reserved for The Dance, dwelling with all the dancers, choreographers, musicians, impresarios and artists who have gone before is Cyril William Beaumont, for whom I have written my book.

Dear Mr B, I hope this will please you.